More Praise for *Killing Marketing*

Joe and Robert take us, once again, to the bleeding edge of marketing . . . but importantly help us understand how to stay there. Their bold thinking, matched only by their bold personalities, jumps off of each page.

—Jonathan Mildenhall,
Chief Marketing Officer, Airbnb

Sometimes the manual needs to be thrown out the door. This book rewrites the rules of marketing, putting content front and center to create value and brand loyalists. Push the envelope, change the approach, and don't be afraid to be disruptive.

—Jeffrey Hayzlett, primetime TV and radio host,
speaker, author and part-time cowboy

Pulizzi and Rose have unlocked the puzzle of what marketing should be in the twenty-first century. Their focus on the two key elements, customers and the income flows those customers create, turns traditional product marketing thinking on its head.

—Don Schultz, Professor Emeritus of Service,
Northwestern University's Medill School

Loaded with ideas to turn content marketing into profit centers. Read it and you'll become a believer, as I have.

—Al Ries, coauthor,
Positioning: The Battle for Your Mind

World renowned marketing experts Pulizzi and Rose partner to author prescriptive advice to help marketing executives transcend purchased media and ascend to owned media prominence.

—Kathy Button Bell, Senior Vice President and
Chief Marketing Officer, Emerson

Killing Marketing is the senior executive handbook for what the marketing function should always have been and now can be.

—Stephanie Losee, Head of Content,
Visa Corporate Communications

Killing Marketing will challenge you to look beyond your known toolkit and change the structure of strategy that will fundamentally and profitably reshape the purpose of marketing in business.

—Timothy McDonough, Vice President Global
Brand Marketing, Moen Incorporated

Killing Marketing is a controversial idea. But controversial marketing is exactly what is needed to profit successfully in the killing crossroads of traditional and new age business.

—Raj Munusamy, Vice President,
Content Marketing & Messaging,
Schneider Electric

Imagine marketing as a profit center, not a cost center. Sound crazy? Nope. This is the blueprint you need to flip marketing on its head, drive innovation, and claim your spot as a business leader.

—Ann Handley, *Wall Street Journal* bestselling
author and Chief Content Officer,
MarketingProfs

Killing Marketing brilliantly demystifies the full implications of content as a preeminent force in customer experience and business transformation in the post-Internet era.

—Carlos Abler, Global Content
Marketing & Strategy Lead, 3M

Buy this book and transform where the marketing budget lives on the balance sheet!

—Rebecca Lieb, analyst, advisor, and author of
Content: The Atomic Particle of Marketing

RIP marketing. It's been real. *Killing Marketing* just put the final nail in your cost center coffin.

—Jason Miller, Global Content
Marketing Leader, LinkedIn

KILLING MARKETING

HOW INNOVATIVE BUSINESSES ARE TURNING
MARKETING COST INTO PROFIT

JOE PULIZZI & ROBERT ROSE

Mc
Graw
Hill
Education

New York   Chicago   San Francisco   Athens
London   Madrid   Mexico City   Milan
New Delhi   Singapore   Sydney   Toronto

1 2 3 4 5 6 7 8 9   LCR   22 21 20 19 18 17

ISBN   978-1-260-02642-9
MHID   1-260-02642-6

e-ISBN   978-1-260-02643-6
e-MHID   1-260-02643-4

*658.8
PUL*

This publication is designed to provide accurate and authoritative information in regard to the subject matter covered. It is sold with the understanding that neither the author nor the publisher is engaged in rendering legal, accounting, securities trading, or other professional services. If legal advice or other expert assistance is required, the services of a competent professional person should be sought.

—*From a Declaration of Principles Jointly Adopted by a Committee of the American Bar Association and a Committee of Publishers and Associations*

McGraw-Hill Education books are available at special quantity discounts to use as premiums and sales promotions or for use in corporate training programs. To contact a representative, please visit the Contact Us pages at www.mhprofessional.com.

Partial cover credit: Joseph Kalinowski

NOV 16 2017

For Elizabeth and Pam—

Well I never had a place that I could call my very own
That's all right, my love, 'cause you're my home

—Billy Joel

Contents

Foreword
BY STEPHANIE LOSEE, HEAD OF CONTENT,
VISA CORPORATE COMMUNICATIONS   ix

Acknowledgments   xi

Introduction   1
BY JOE PULIZZI

Chapter 1 | Killing Marketing   17
BY ROBERT ROSE

Chapter 2 | Return on Audience   41
BY ROBERT ROSE

Chapter 3 | Media Marketing   63
BY JOE PULIZZI

Chapter 4 | The Revenue Model   87
BY JOE PULIZZI

Chapter 5 | The Marketing Media Savings Model   119
BY ROBERT ROSE

Chapter 6 | First Steps on the Road to Killing Marketing   139
BY ROBERT ROSE

Chapter 7 | The One Media Model   155
BY JOE PULIZZI

Chapter 8 | Today: The Beginning   183
BY JOE PULIZZI

Chapter 9 | What Now: Lessons Learned
Along the Transformation   209
BY ROBERT ROSE

Chapter 10 | The Future of Marketing   225
BY ROBERT ROSE

Index   247

Foreword

When Joe and Robert first approached me with the idea behind *Killing Marketing*, I initially thought about the phenomenon of brands monetizing their content by becoming full-on media companies.

I was thinking of Red Bull, because we all do. Red Bull was an early example of content marketing leadership—of using content to build audiences and then profiting from those relationships. Content had turned Red Bull's business upside down to such a degree that the company claimed it was no longer an energy drink company that published media, but a media company that sold energy drinks.

The marketers I talked to about the coming of content were not only dubious of the Red Bull model; they found it unappetizing. Why would chief marketing officers (CMOs) want to turn their brands into media companies? Media's business model was collapsing. If it weren't collapsing, we wouldn't be in this damn "advertising-doesn't-work-anymore-so-now-I-have-to-deal-with-creating-content" pickle in the first place.

But I've come to understand that the potential for content marketing to transform the business goes far beyond thinking and acting like a media company. It's about realizing that our assumptions about what marketing can achieve might be wrong.

Several years after Red Bull's business flip, just about every CMO and founder I know has established some kind of content creation function; yet most have done so reluctantly and with a certain degree of resignation. It has to be because they're missing what Joe and Robert provide in *Killing Marketing*: a blueprint for how companies can pull off their own Red Bull coup, in whatever form that might take.

Each organization can use content to achieve the CMO's holy grail—marketing as a true profit center—in ways that are unique to each business. Interactions with customers spurred by content can inspire the development of new product lines. They can inform pivots in corporate strategy. Shifts in brand messaging. Ripples from customer ground zero all the way to the C-suite.

Killing Marketing is the senior executive handbook for what the marketing function should always have been and now can be. Content transformed Red Bull into a media company. Content will transform your business in another way. At the very least, it will serve as the mechanism that finally elevates marketing from a tax on the business to a true business itself.

—*Stephanie Losee, Head of Content,*
Visa Corporate Communications

Acknowledgments

From Joe Pulizzi—

To the entire Content Marketing Institute staff, especially Clare McDermott for her amazing interview powers and "JK" Kalinowski for his design prowess. I'm proud to call all of you my friends.

To Jim McDermott (my mentor), my amazing parents Tony and Terry Pulizzi, and my Coolio friends in Cleveland, Ohio, who continue to keep life interesting.

To my boys, Joshua and Adam. Whatever you do, be optimistic, and even in the worst of times, you'll find the light. I'm proud of you both.

To my best friend and soul mate, Pam. Most!

And to Mr. Robert Rose. You've made this journey more fun than I could have ever imagined. Here's to our next journey.

Phil 4:13

From Robert Rose—

To everyone at the Content Marketing Institute, you all make me better. Every. Single. Day. To Clare McDermott, especially, thank you for being the muse, to pull the stories from amazing people.

To Cathy McKnight and Dr. Tim Walters, you are my friends, and my compass for ideas. I find true north in your counsel.

To my family, Laura, Elizabeth, Daisy, and Bill, you are my spiritual foundation. You are the reason why.

And to the good gentleman from Cleveland, who is a guiding light, a conspirator of laughs, a sounding board of sanity, and simply proof in the world that nice guys finish first. Joe Pulizzi—I am simply a better man for knowing you, but I'm truly blessed to be able to call you my friend.

Now . . . where are my shoes?

Introduction

BY
JOE
PULIZZI

There is an epidemic failure within the game to understand what is really happening. . . . They are asking all the wrong questions.

—Peter Brand in the movie *Moneyball*

It ain't what you don't know that gets you into trouble. It's what you know for sure that just ain't so.

—Mostly credited to Mark Twain

In the 1970s, Israeli psychologists Danny Kahneman and Amos Tversky wrote a research paper titled "Belief in the Law of Small Numbers." The findings were that even professional academics mistook a very small part for the whole when making decisions. For example, even though flipping a coin is always a 50/50 proposition, if a subject were to flip it 100 times, but the first two times turned up heads, the subject would believe that the majority of flips would turn up heads—at least higher than the true probability. This is also known as the "gambler's fallacy," where in roulette we see red or black running hot, and we begin to think that red or black is more likely to occur, when statistically it's not.

As human beings, the more we see something, the more this becomes our reality, regardless of whether our sample size is too small to draw any real conclusions.

• • •

In the mid-1980s, Don Redelmeier was assigned to Sunnybrook Hospital just outside Toronto to serve as a check against certain hospital decisions. Specifically, Redelmeier was brought in to question each doctor's diagnosis and provide feedback as to the probability the doctor was correct.

Obviously, this was something that the Sunnybrook doctors were not fans of . . . at first. Where did a generalist (Redelmeier) from the trauma center get the right to question a qualified physician?

But Redelmeier, and others like him, found that doctors "had exaggerated confidence based on their expert experience." Simply put, doctors would see problems and solutions around their core expertise, and would oftentimes ignore other signals where they were not as familiar.

The problem was not what doctors didn't know; it's what they knew that would get them into trouble.

• • •

In November of last year I took my son Adam to a high school open house. While he was taking a few of the sample classes during the morning sessions, I was doing the same with a group of parents. My first class of the day was called the Theory of Knowledge.

The assignment was simple: view a painting of a building and discuss what you "know" about the painting. Our group tried to discern when it was created, whether it was real or fictitious, and, if it was real, was it a famous place?

Once the discussion was completed, the instructor told us that the painter was Adolf Hitler. From that moment on, everything about the conversation was immediately altered. A few people even became emotional upon hearing this information. The truth was, once the majority of the class found out this one piece of information, they could no longer view the painting as a piece of art.

What the class "knew" could never be undone and would affect their perception of that piece of art, and perhaps others like it, forever.

DOES WHAT WE KNOW HOLD US BACK IN MARKETING?

No, this is not a psychology, medical, or art history book, but the previous examples are definitely applicable. For the past 20 years, Robert and I have worked with CEOs, chief marketing officers, VPs of sales and marketing, and marketing practitioners from brands around the world. In each case, some part of their marketing and/or sales process was broken.

We go in, we analyze, we advise, and (hopefully) we compel these marketers and sales professionals to fix what they can with the resources they have. But what we've realized in the past few years has become, to say the least, disturbing.

Combined, this book, *Killing Marketing*, is our sixth such effort. Normally when creating the work product such as a book, we start with the answer to a question. For example, in my 2013 book *Epic Content Marketing*, I talk about how marketers can build loyal and profitable relationships with customers by delivering consistently valuable content in order to drive sales. In 2015, Robert (with Carla Johnson) wrote the book *Experiences: The 7th Era of Marketing*, which outlines an approach on how content-driven experiences can be created, managed, scaled, promoted, and measured in today's business environment.

This book, however, does not start with an answer . . . it begins with questions . . . questions that Robert and I are desperate to find the answers to.

- What if what we've been taught or experienced in marketing doesn't show us the full picture?

- What if we've limited our view of marketing to one area (what we know), and that is not allowing us to see the full potential of what can be accomplished (what we do not know yet)?

- What if placing marketing solely in the marketing department is killing the approach of marketing as a strategic business process?

In other words, what if everything we *know* to be true about marketing is actually what's holding back our business?

THE DAY HOLLYWOOD CHANGED

Let's try to make this more tangible with a popular movie example.

American Graffiti, still today, is one of the most profitable movies of all time. The film, made on a budget of less than $1 million, grossed over $140 million at the box office. After the success of *Graffiti*, director George Lucas was in demand, and he started pitching his next venture, a science fiction movie series called *Star Wars*, to Hollywood studios.

At the time, Hollywood was seeing a number of science fiction flops, and the industry did not see *Star Wars* as a bankable concept. Ultimately, 20th Century Fox decided to take a chance on the film. Still, the executives at Fox were sure the movie was going to be a flop and decided to let Lucas pass on an additional $500,000 directing fee in exchange for full licensing and merchandising rights. The studio believed it had just saved a half a million dollars with no downside.

From 1977 to 2015 (before the Disney release of *Star Wars: The Force Awakens*), *Star Wars* movies pulled in just over $5 billion in ticket sales. During that same period, merchandising sales were $12 billion.

That's right . . . 20th Century Fox sold off merchandising rights to George Lucas for pennies and lost out on a vast majority of the franchise revenue. It believed, as most of Hollywood insiders did at the time, that you make money from movies on ticket sales. Period.

George Lucas looked at the business in an entirely different way, and changed the industry forever.

Is it possible that the majority of CEOs and chief marketing officers are looking at marketing based on their own limited references (what they believe to be true about marketing), and not seeing the full potential (what they may not know), like the Hollywood insiders did? Are they killing their marketing from the inside without being aware of it?

THE PURPOSE OF MARKETING

In one of his 70 books on marketing, famed marketing professor Philip Kotler explained that the "mantra of marketing was

CCDVTP." This acronym suggested that the core function of marketing should be to:

> Create, Communicate, and Deliver Value
> to a Target market at a Profit.

Now, of course, the "profit" that Kotler speaks about is the idea that marketing should ultimately drive more sales of product than it should create costs in order to facilitate those sales. This is what marketers call the return on investment (ROI) of marketing.

Most of our marketing in the past 50 years has revolved around advertising, or renting space in channels to garner attention and, hopefully, change consumer behavior. But over the past decade, innovative enterprises have found a "new" way to deliver value to their target markets. This approach, called *content marketing*, is where organizations create relevant and compelling content, gear it toward specific audience groups, and then, over time, see positive behavior changes in the audience that, ultimately, are profitable to the business. Some organizations, like John Deere, have been employing content marketing for over 100 years, while to others the approach is relatively new. Regardless, the goals remain the same.

In general, enterprises create and distribute non-product-related content to impact their business in three ways:

- Increase revenue (sales goal, or winning customers)

- Save costs (savings goal, or creating customers at a lower cost)

- Create more loyal customers (retention goal, or keeping customers)

But, recently, there's a new approach that has businesses reevaluating the entire function of marketing.

A FOURTH MODEL:
MARKETING AS PROFIT CENTER

I had an opportunity to hear Robert Sperl, editorial director of Red Bull's magazine *Red Bulletin*, explain the origin of Red Bull Media House. In 2005, the beverage giant was a major sponsor of Formula 1 racing. It had a simple goal for one of the races: to deliver a printed guide with the race results to exiting fans immediately following the race.

Prior to each race, the Red Bull editorial team gathered insider stories about the drivers and fun facts about the history of each race, and then assembled and printed the bulk of each magazine before the race began. To complete the magazine and add the race results, they lugged a one-ton Heidelberg press to each track. As soon as the race was over, they quickly printed the results on the Heidelberg and distributed the magazines to attendees as they were leaving the race—an astounding feat done in almost record time.

Two years later, Red Bull decided to evolve the race publication into a men's lifestyle magazine. It launched what became *Red Bulletin* in five countries, with 70 percent international and 30 percent localized content. Today, *Red Bulletin* magazine is published in five languages and is distributed in 10 countries. Red Bull prints and distributes over two million copies each month, including 550,000 mailed to paid subscribers.

The *Red Bulletin* is not measured by how many Red Bull cans it sells, or by how it persuades Red Bull customers to buy and drink more. It is measured just like a media company—Red Bull

Media House enters into initiatives that are profitable on their own merit, just like the *Washington Post*, CNN, or the *Financial Times*.

Today, Red Bull Media House is one of the world's most successful media companies. What started as a simple magazine has evolved into TV series, documentaries, world-class events, a music studio, and merchandising, and Red Bull even licenses its content to traditional media companies like the *New York Times*.

While other enterprises were dabbling in media as, at best, a side project, how did Red Bull see this opportunity? Simple— Robert Sperl, and the majority of the other members of the Red Bull media staff, came from the publishing and media industry. Like George Lucas, the members of the Red Bull content team saw the business model in front of them as a natural progression, instead of looking past it as so many marketers did before them.

Today, the Red Bull model is being replicated in varying degrees across the business spectrum. Business-to-business (B2B) companies, business-to-consumer (B2C) companies, and even not-for-profits are starting to realize that as they focus on creating valuable and engaging content, a new model appears: marketing as a profit center.

Can we actually move marketing from the cost line of the financials to the revenue line? Can marketing actually serve multiple business models?

Our book—*Killing Marketing*—presents an entirely new business model for marketing: one that leverages the disruptive forces facing marketing and advertising, as it also fundamentally changes the purpose of marketing in the business. Like the Hollywood insiders falling down on *Star Wars*' merchandising revenue, we believe marketers are, in most cases, blind to this new opportunity.

A few are starting to see that, to be successful, we need to kill our old marketing beliefs to discover a new model.

Cloud CRM giant Salesforce holds an event in San Francisco every year called Dreamforce. It is one of the most valuable physical events in the world, drawing in over 150,000 people and hundreds of sponsors each year.

Johnson & Johnson operates BabyCenter.com as a completely separate division of the company. BabyCenter reaches more than 45 million parents a month from every corner of the globe through its 11 owned and operated properties in 9 different languages. In the United States, 8 of every 10 mothers use BabyCenter.

LEGO's *The LEGO Movie* was created as a for-profit initiative. On a $60 million budget, worldwide grosses of the movie totaled nearly a half a billion dollars.

These examples are just the tip of the iceberg, often barely noticeable to marketers or even dismissed as irregularities or luck. But in the near future, this model will be the rule, not the exception, for every innovative company on the planet.

DRIVING VALUE OUTSIDE OF PRODUCTS

According to SiriusDecisions, there is a 1 in 25 chance to reach a C-level executive through outbound marketing. There must be a better way.

We're beginning to see the signs of that better way.

In 2016, both Pepsi and Mondelez announced the launch of media divisions. In both cases, the marketing leaders at these organizations talked openly about a portion of their media being self-sustaining or even profitable.

A few months later, electronics manufacturing powerhouse and Fortune 500 enterprise Arrow Electronics acquired a number of B2B media brands from UBM, one of the largest media and event companies in the world, and Hearst. Not only has Arrow purchased amazingly valuable subscriber lists and editorial talent, but it also purchased stand-alone marketing that is profitable unto itself.

Red Bull, Johnson & Johnson, and Arrow Electronics still market their products like other organizations, including advertising and traditional public relations. But these enterprises, through their content-driven and audience-building initiatives, drive value outside the day-to-day products they sell, and are monetizing it directly. They are, in every sense of the word, "media" companies.

Of course these initiatives sell more cans, more baby formula, and more electrical components. The delivery of amazingly helpful content keeps customers longer, keeps them buying more, and even helps new customers close faster. The engagement in the content reveals deep insight about customer behavior and leads to the development of new products and services. All that, and the marketing pays for itself and even generates a profit for the business.

This is the future of IBM, of General Motors, of Cisco Systems—creating owned media that not only can generate more leads and opportunities, but is so good that the marketing pays for itself.

WHAT *KILLING MARKETING* WILL DELIVER

For the last decade, Robert and I have watched this transformation begin. Now, routinely, brands have as compelling a publication as the traditional media companies do in any particular industry. Enterprises have begun to acquire media companies, launch specific content brands, and sell advertising, training, and subscriptions as part of that strategy.

Traditional advertising, direct marketing, digital marketing, and even social media are all transforming. And all of them point toward a landscape where brands go directly to consumers, rather than relying on the gatekeepers of traditional media to get there. The only thing that prevented this in the past was the difficulty of getting in front of an audience.

Alexis Ohanian, cofounder of Reddit, says it best: "For centuries, invention was limited to those who had access to the means of production and access to labor. Today, you can simply create and present [distribute] your ideas online. Granted, if it's that easy for you, it's that easy for everyone." With the disruption of the Internet and digital content, access to audiences has been democratized. *All that now remains is a race for the competency and the talent.* Marketing, as we know it, is slowly dying, and most marketing executives don't see it.

Killing Marketing is both a visionary and pragmatic look at how businesses are beginning to make this transformation. We illuminate the road map for how brands will:

- Acquire the competency to transform some portion of their marketing operation to work as a media company.

- Integrate a content-as-value operation into traditional marketing efforts and invest in this new operation over time.

- Create best practices for how businesses attract and retain audiences, and compete against both their normal competitors *and* the traditional media companies that also target their customers.

- Formulate a process for creating a paid and earned media strategy that will actually be fueled by a profitable *owned* media strategy.

■ Learn from dozens of businesses how to develop a repeatable process for success.

THINK DIFFERENT

Whether you are a CEO at a Fortune 500 company, are the VP of marketing at a midsize enterprise, or own the smallest of small businesses, this book is for those who want (and probably need) to think differently about how to grow your business—especially in an era when anyone, anywhere, can copy your product or service. Whatever your title or role, if you are part of the sales and marketing process to generate revenue, this book was created for you.

Your job, as a marketing professional, is to push away the biases you have and start to look at marketing as not just driving demand. You have to look at it like you are a foreigner looking at a new country for the first time. Ask yourself, what else is content doing? And then ask yourself, what else can content do?

Ultimately, you have to make the decision to kill how you market so that you can take advantage of an entirely new model.

The marketing skills of tomorrow are equal parts marketing and publishing. To survive, we need to understand both, and the business model that is born from that mixture. We're hoping this will be a fun and enlightening journey for you.

To assist you in your mission, we've included the following at the end of each chapter:

■ **Profitable Insights.** These are issues and takeaways to keep in mind to help you think differently about your sales, marketing, and communication.

■ **Profitable Resources.** This book draws from literally thousands of books, articles, podcasts, blog posts, movies, presentations, and comments from colleagues and influencers. Any of those resources that helped a specific chapter come together will be included at the end of each chapter.

Thank you for deciding to take this epic journey with us. Good luck!

Patience, persistence and perspiration make an unbeatable combination for success.

—Napoleon Hill

Profitable Insights

■ Over the past 20 years marketing has fundamentally changed, and yet most organizations (and marketers) are marketing exactly the same way.

■ The most innovative companies in the world have identified this change and have started to move marketing from a cost (or a tax on the business) to an actual profit center.

■ To succeed with this new "media marketing" business model, you have to forget what you know about what marketing is supposed to be and look at it with fresh eyes.

Profitable Resources

- Amos Tversky and Daniel Kahneman, "Belief in the Law of Small Numbers," *Psychological Bulletin* 76, no. 2 (August 1971): 105–110.

- Michael Lewis, *The Undoing Project* (W. W. Norton & Company, 2016).

- "Franchises: Star Wars," BoxOfficeMojo.com, accessed May 23, 2017, http://www.boxofficemojo.com/franchises/chart/?id=starwars.htm.

- "The Real Force Behind Star Wars: How George Lucas Built an Empire," TheHollywoodReporter.com, accessed May 23, 2017, http://www.hollywoodreporter.com/news/george-lucas-star-wars-288513.

- "The Ingenious Path George Lucas Took to Making Billions off Star Wars," BusinessInsider.com, accessed May 23, 2017, http://www.businessinsider.com/how-star-wars-made-george-lucas-a-billionaire-2015-12.

- "How Star Wars Changed Film Marketing Forever," AMA.org, accessed May 23, 2017, https://www.ama.org/publications/MarketingNews/Pages/the-history-of-marketing-star-wars.aspx.

- "We Can Say that CCDVTP Is a New Marketing Theory (Philip Kotler)," bayt.com, accessed May 23, 2017, https://www.bayt.com/en/specialties/q/42325/we-can-say-that-quot-ccdvtp-quot-is-a-new-marketing-theory-philip-kotler/.

- "Mondelez Makes Moves to Look More Like a Media Company," WSJ.com, accessed May 23, 2017, https://www.wsj.com/articles/mondelez-makes-moves-to-look-more-like-a-media-company-1464692402.

- "The LEGO Movie," boxofficemojo.com, accessed May 23, 2017, http://www.boxofficemojo.com/movies/?id=lego.htm.

- Alexis Ohanian, *Without Their Permission* (Business Plus, 2013).

1

Killing Marketing

BY
**ROBERT
ROSE**

*Most companies don't fail because they are wrong; they fail
because they don't commit themselves. The greatest danger
is in standing still.*

—Andy Grove, CEO, Intel

Quick, kill it before it lays eggs

—Popular Internet meme

D id you know that the plane crash is an invention?

It is. It joins the automobile crash, burned microwave
popcorn, and the hard drive fail as some of the more notable
inventions of the twentieth century.

This idea comes from Paul Virilio, a French cultural theorist,
urbanist, and "philosopher of speed." Virilio's concept refers to
technology and how the invention of any new technology also
simultaneously invents the disaster resulting from that technology.
As he put it, "When you invent the ship, you also invent the shipwreck; when you invent the plane you also invent the plane crash."

All technology innovations, whether a ship, a plane, microwave popcorn, a computer hard drive, or even new approaches in business, have corresponding disasters that have consequences for us as humans. And it is an excellent metaphor for where we are with the practice of marketing today.

In the introduction to this book, Joe asked an important question: **"What if everything we *know* to be true about marketing is actually what's holding back our business?"**

What if we finally realized that we've invented the shipwreck of marketing?

Shouldn't we look? Shouldn't we redesign it?

What if we killed the marketing we know—so that we might reinvent something new?

It's certainly no great revelation at this point that the marketing and media landscape has fundamentally changed over the last 18 years. As Joe and I wrote in *Managing Content Marketing*, our first book together, in 2011:

> We're all in agreement that the influences of the explosive growth of the mobile and social Web are creating seismic shifts in all areas of business. We watch, as the Web threatens the existence of entire content-oriented sectors such as periodicals, newspapers, book stores, record companies, and broadcast television. . . . Entire job categories such as HR benefits manager, travel agent, librarian, journalist, photographer, videographer, and Web designer are going the way of the linotypist, stenographer, and elevator operator.
>
> The social and mobile Web has completely changed the speed, efficiency, and ease with which consumers can engage with each other and has had a tremendous impact on brands. This new need for consumer engagement now correlates to every single aspect of our business. Marketing now influences how our salespeople sell, accountants account, researchers

research, developers develop, service people service, and even how leaders lead.

It's funny: As marketers, we've been so keenly aware of how the world has changed around us. But we haven't changed marketing at all.

Now, to be clear—we don't mean the *purpose* of marketing, or why it exists. Rather, we mean the *function* of marketing and how it works. The purpose of the business, as Peter Drucker said 60 years ago, is "*to create and keep a customer.*" And as he also said, "Marketing and innovation produce results; all the rest are costs. Marketing is the distinguishing, unique function of the business." And as the unique and distinguishing function of the business, the purpose of marketing is then to be that which creates and keeps customers. Joe and I agree with that wholeheartedly.

The only question is, *how is that done?*

Even with the fundamental changes in the world in which we live, we still haven't changed the *function* of marketing.

HOW DID WE GET HERE?

One of the things that's often misstated in this digital content and media revolution is that the creation of content has become democratized. This isn't true. The *creation* of original content isn't any easier today than it was before Gutenberg invented his printing press. It still takes specialized talent and time to focus on quality. What *has been democratized* to the point of overload is the production and distribution of content. What used to take special skills, expensive tools, and large, continuous investment in distribution now can be done ostensibly by anyone, with off-the-shelf tools and for free.

Interestingly, and paradoxically, as the production and distribution of content has become more commoditized, this means that the value of original, high-quality content continues to increase. The ability to garner and hold attention from an audience with original content becomes increasingly valuable to any endeavor that desires that the audience do something, whether that be to buy, donate, vote, become loyal, or spread the message.

In today's world, we as consumers have tools that filter through the noise for just exactly what we want. And once we consumers find and trust the source of the things we like, we tend to begin to rely on it as a continual source of that information or entertainment.

You can see this trend happening across the media landscape:

- HBO's over-the-top service, HBO Now, is still only a small portion of its approximately 50 million subscribers in traditional cable. But it has added 2 million subscribers in less than two years and is accelerating. In 2017, HBO planned to add more than 600 hours of original programming.

- Netflix, which started as a DVD rental service, has now gone from approximately 27 million subscribers in 2012 to more than 60 million subscribers in five years. Consider that within the next few years more than 50 percent of Netflix's content will be original productions.

- In a transformed news media environment, complete with "fake news" and mistrusted outlets, brands such as the *New York Times*, the *Washington Post*, the *Atlantic*, and others are seeing an exponential increase in subscription rates.

- Amazon, the world's largest retailer, has launched Amazon Studios and will spend more than $2.6 billion on original content for its Amazon Prime service in 2017.

| Figure 1.1 | Owned media value curve |

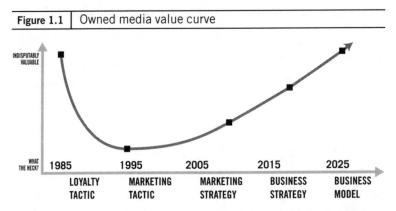

The perceived value of owned media content decreased precipitously as technology democratized production and distribution. However, the importance of acquisition, retention, and relationship with audiences has caused a recent surge in perceived value and an opportunity for a renaissance in marketing.

And we can see this trend happening in the value of original business content as well. When we plot the strategic value of content over time, we get a graph like the one shown in Figure 1.1. As the figure depicts, the perceived value of content started very high and then plummeted as production and distribution costs decreased with new technologies. Now, that value has begun to increase sharply as content becomes a more meaningful way to connect with audiences and buyers. Let's walk through each of the phases.

ORIGINAL CONTENT: THE LOYALTY TACTIC

In the pre-digital, pre-web world, the value of original content to the enterprise was relatively high. Why? Because every piece of content was a considered purchase for a business. As we mentioned, it wasn't the creation of original content that was so expensive; it was the production and distribution of the content. Whether it was a print ad, a brochure, a billboard, or a consumer magazine, the cost was something that you needed specialists for. In the early 1980s (pre-digital), the average cost of producing a four-color, full-page advertisement was approximately $8,000. That is approximately $20,000 in 2017 money. Today, if you'd like to produce a four-color full-page advertisement, according to experts it could cost you somewhere close to $0 (assuming you legally license software) to open Adobe Photoshop and do it yourself. Or you might go to an Internet-based, on-demand solution like 99Designs.com and pay $200. Or you might contract with a freelancer or agency directly and pay anywhere between $1,500 and $30,000 on the high end.

Then, distribution was an even more expensive aspect of original content. The only means of distributing content were to leverage your own mailing lists, get the content placed (for purchase) in a retail outlet, or "rent" a media company's access to audiences.

So, the cost of original content (read "risk") was high. And when we look at owned media, we can see a definite trend. As Joe and I have written in our previous books, the idea of creating owned media for audiences isn't a new idea. It's been around for hundreds of years. But pre-digital owned media was most consistently used as a loyalty tactic. These were the magazines that you'd find in the airline seat pocket. This was the association magazine you received for being a member. These were the *extra* content-driven experiences you received *after* you became a customer. Why? Because at that point, the business knew that you would actually receive it. The company had your address or your phone number. Or the publication was quite literally dropped in the bag of the store you just shopped in. The company knew how to reach you, and thus the loyalty tactic was the one approach that had a low enough risk to justify producing the expensive content. It was a distribution channel that the brand controlled.

Then, as shown in Figure 1.1, the perceived value of content dropped precipitously as we entered the digital age, first driven by the word processing and desktop publishing revolution of the 1980s and 1990s, and then of course by the Internet and World Wide Web phenomenon of the early 2000s. Suddenly, you could produce your original content using prosumer (or enterprise) technology, and the cost of both production and distribution dropped. Thus the risk came way down, and businesses' appetite for producing more and more content went up.

CONTENT: THE MARKETING TACTIC

The early 2000s was a time when businesses decided to *go around* the traditional media. Digital technology enabled us to circumvent traditional media. We could use the technology at hand to build our own content destinations on the web. We could message customers directly using email, and then subsequently social media. We could deploy technologies to build communities. The only challenge? To be found. The mandate was to create optimized online destinations that were easy to find by Internet search engines. Traffic would be cheap (or even free), and we could reap the benefit by publishing as much content as we could to our websites.

And so the risk, and the perceived value of content, plummeted—both in the production costs and in the value that the company placed on it. Owned media content became a simple marketing tactic. We gave responsibility for our websites to the "young people," our interns and our nieces and nephews. Businesses created separate digital marketing groups with the sole purpose of creating more and more digital reach and frequency.

The separate groups, though, were given scant investment. The "real value" of media was still held in the traditional production and distribution channels. A famous quote from the early 2000s was that we don't want to "trade analog dollars for digital dimes."

But businesses leapt with great vigor at every new channel and content feed they could—and chased the technology voraciously trying to apply the classic rules of sales and marketing to the new digitized world. The theory was that digital content was always going to be cheaper to produce, easier to distribute, and more efficient than anything that came before. So, why not produce as much of it as we possibly can?

But it stopped working. It became more and more difficult to achieve results. What happened? The rules changed.

People started to consume even more media every day, jumping to more than 10 hours every single day. And we spend most of that on social networks. Facebook alone now commands an average of 50 minutes of a person's day.

And the tsunami of content compelled businesses to change their model again. Google changed its algorithms to reward "quality content" to try to improve the value of search to advertisers. Facebook and the other social platforms decided that organic reach wasn't going to be something attained for free any longer. New media suddenly looked a lot like old media—protective of the relationship with their audience and loathe to simply give access away. Suddenly, *quality* became the word. And forward-leaning marketers realized that they too could compete in this environment. They no longer had to depend on traditional media for production and distribution. Businesses with smart marketing could leverage inexpensive production and distribution and aggregate their own audiences. The challenge to these marketers: not only did they need to create original content *for* the media—they had to *become* the media. The pressure for value began to increase, because this transformation required something they didn't have. Talent.

CONTENT: THE MARKETING STRATEGY

As we moved out of the Great Recession of 2008–2010, marketers began to see the increasing value of original owned media content as a means of creating greater trust with customers. Forward-leaning brands created publishing houses, producing original content in multiple forms. For example, General Electric created multiple digital magazines including *GE Reports*, which reaches 300,000 readers, putting it on par with many consumer-oriented science magazines. Another example is American Express's OPEN Forum, an educational source and community where small business owners can learn from business thought leaders and each other. This forum reaches more than a million unique visitors per month—and now represents the source for 50 percent of the company's small business credit card applications.

Both B2B and B2C brands recognized the power of content as a marketing strategy. Big companies such as General Electric, LEGO, Kraft/Heinz, IBM, Cisco, P&G, Coca-Cola, and Capital One all began creating owned media publications as a means of building strategic relationships with audiences. A renewed interest in "custom publishing" with an emphasis on digital began to provide media companies with new business models.

The Cannes Lion Awards, one of advertising's most prestigious events—and one that has been held since the 1940s—added "Branded Content" as a new category in 2012.

Content began to be referred to as a strategy. Content marketing, as a practice, grew in importance to marketing. It went from tactic to valuable marketing strategy. As Joe wrote in 2008, in his first book *Get Content Get Customers* with Newt Barrett:

> Marketing organizations are now realizing that they can create content whose quality is equal to or better than what many media companies are producing. . . .
>
> By delivering content that is vital and relevant to your target market, you will begin to take on an important role in your customers' lives. This applies to your online, print, and in-person communications. And this is the same role that newspapers, magazines, TV, radio, conferences, workshops, and Web sites have played in the past. Now it's time for your organization to play that role.

And so the value began to increase, but so too did the risk and the cost of acquiring new talent. The brands that chose to play the role found the inevitable challenges and realizations. High-quality, original content creation is difficult. To be successful means looking at marketing through an entirely different lens. This strategy was tempting, but original content required talent that the business didn't have, culture shifts that the business didn't want to make, and new measurement, governance, and processes that the business didn't understand.

And this leads us to where we are today.

CONTENT: THE BUSINESS STRATEGY

In 2015, Joe released his book *Content Inc.*, in which he told of a different business model—one where companies build an audience first and then determine what products should be sold:

In the future, thousands of businesses around the globe will be leveraging a Content Inc. go-to-market strategy. Why? Because having a singular focus on audience, and building a loyal audience directly, gives you the best understanding of what products ultimately make the most sense to sell.

In my previous book *Experiences*, written with Carla Johnson and released in 2015, we wrote of the coming evolution when we said:

> Content—and the exponentially increasing quantities that every organization produces—affects our marketing strategy and should be dealt with as a component of that strategy throughout the enterprise. . . . Content will affect business—it's just a matter of "how," not "if."

This is the state of owned media and marketing today. The potential value of owned media to the organization is increasing rapidly. Those forward-leaning businesses that have been along the curve, like Kraft Heinz, General Electric, and Johnson & Johnson, are no longer willing to simply accept the idea that they must continually rent access to audiences. They are no longer looking at social media as solely a means to try to organically build a community of loyal customers. They won't accept that content is simply a short-term investment meant to supplement advertising. They are looking at how owned media experiences—and the audiences they build—can add multiple lines of value to their businesses, and thus change not only their marketing approach but their *entire business strategy.*

We will talk about this through the examples in this book, as it's where we are today. But there is yet another step. And getting there means that marketing, as we currently know it, must die.

CONTENT: THE BUSINESS MODEL

As we move to 2020 and beyond, a new function will begin to permeate the function of marketing. **It is the strategic use of content that will not only build audiences and drive the creation and retention of customers; it will do so at a profit.** It will transform marketing as we know it today into something new. It will evolve the entire practice of marketing and can move some or all of the functions of marketing from cost center to profit center.

As Joe indicated in the introduction to this book, "This is the future of IBM, of General Motors, of Cisco Systems—creating owned media that not only can generate more leads and opportunities, but is so good that the marketing pays for itself."

But as I said—in order to do that, we have to be willing to kill the marketing we know.

KILLING MARKETING

If we said that the marketing leader in business should be of the same stature as one would regard the most advanced practitioners of art, science, law, and/or medicine, most people would probably laugh.

Today, while perhaps sexy on the outside, marketing for most businesses is in a depressed, average state.

Marketing is the activity that most companies wish they didn't have to do. For many businesses, it is simply a "tax" on the system, and the focus is putting as little investment into it as possible. Most businesses are striving for what I call "minimum viable marketing." One CEO I spoke with directly said, *"Marketing is a tax. Therefore I'm going to cheat sometimes, cut it frequently, and always use all my power in order to pay as little for it as possible."* For many business-to-business (B2B) companies, there really isn't a strategic marketing leader in the organization. It's simply a collection of people who do marketing-like things. The marketing team may report to sales as an "internal agency." Or if there is a leader—the leader's sole focus is to pour more leads and opportunities onto sales teams.

On the business-to-consumer (B2C) side, marketing is apt to be taken more seriously, but it's still "the department that simply finds ever more clever ways to dispose of what the company makes." And as the quote from marketing legend and professor Philip Kotler says, *"Marketing is not the art of finding clever ways to dispose of what you make. Marketing is the art of creating genuine customer value. It is the art of helping your customer become better off."*

Now, this isn't to say that there aren't some firms that have clearly defined ideas of what marketing is and how it works. Companies like P&G, General Electric, LEGO, and Apple have excelled in producing some of the world's leading strategies. In fact, P&G is legendary for its approach to marketing training. P&G marketing alumni include former Microsoft CEO Steve Ballmer, HP CEO Meg Whitman, General Electric CEO Jeff Immelt, current Estée Lauder CEO Fabrizio Freda, and Unilever CEO Paul Polman.

But for every P&G or General Electric, there are hundreds of thousands of other companies that are struggling to identify the strategic nature of their marketing efforts. The rapid growth of digitization and new business practices have simply swamped these companies, to the point where today's marketing departments are chasing technology in order to try to digitize traditional processes rather than creating new strategies and figuring out how to digitize them.

The basic practices of marketing have not changed in 60 years. Most marketing departments, despite the fact that they now have a twin department called "digital marketing" these days, are still focused on the same functions. They create, run, and iterate temporal campaigns across traditional (read "expensive") media flights and hope for improving results on getting their message to resonate in front of rented audiences. Then, simultaneously, they support other efforts—from sales to e-commerce to public relations and other departments with creative assets that can feed those departments' time-based campaigns. As we said in the beginning of the chapter, this has always been the job of marketing—maximizing the reach of our message across campaigns and minimizing the frequency with which we have to do it.

But its efficacy—or at least the perception of efficacy—continues to degrade over time. In a recent interview in *The Marketing Journal*, Bernie Jaworski, the Drucker Chair in Management and the Liberal Arts at the Drucker School of Management for Clairmont Graduate University, said:

> I think there's a lot of ambiguity about where and how marketing can best add value to the organization. 50% of the CMO's role is not marketing. Furthermore, in many situations companies have lost "control" of their story.

Consider two trends. In the 2016–2017 CMO Spend Survey, research firm Gartner found that marketing budgets increased to 12 percent of company revenue. This was the third consecutive year of budget increases. The biggest increases were in digital, where content, digital commerce, and digital advertising were the biggest categories.

Should we see this as good news? Well, possibly—but you can also make a strong argument that this is throwing good money after bad. Sure, we've adopted the new technologies, learned the new language of speaking in 140 characters, become customer-centric, and diversified our investments to address the fragmentation of audiences. But as has been the case for more than 100 years, our marketing investment is still almost entirely predicated on our current relationship with the media.

Marketing departments are still wholly dependent on the relationship that media companies have with audiences in order to periodically gain access to them and put our message in front of them.

The investment math is very simple. **We try to *maximize* the reach of our message (the thing we want to persuade audiences with) and try to minimize the frequency (or the inherent cost) of doing that very thing.** In other words, our job is to reduce the friction of the cost of reaching and influencing an audience. And we've used the same approach to doing that since mass media began. Whether it was print, radio, television, public relations, SEO, digital advertising, or native advertising, it was all about maximizing the reach while minimizing the cost of frequency.

Unfortunately, this speed and technology has evolved marketing into much more of a day-trading investment rather than long-term value investing. Businesses now routinely expect return on their investment in months, weeks, days, or even minutes. We've invented real-time marketing where technology and research companies promise to "unlock your data" so as to provide you with return on investment in "real time." Marketing departments are now fascinated with predictive analytics, artificial intelligence, and machine learning—where we can theoretically know what the results will be before we even begin. Now that's return on investment!

Thoughtful strategy has given way to execution. Deep insight has given way to failing fast. Innovation has given way to acceptable inefficiency. Consider this: in 2014, the Internet Advertising Bureau (IAB)—the standard-bearer of digital advertising—stated that because of ad blocking technology, advertising click fraud, and other technology issues, marketers should "aim for 70 percent" viewability on their ads. This would be the new standard of acceptable viewability of an advertisement.

Think about that for a moment. As marketers, we have come to a place where, as renters of media access, we have done the calculus and determined that a 30 percent "tax" on a media buy is *less expensive* than doing something completely different. Perhaps this is the reason we're seeing digital ad budgets go up. *It's not that it's more effective; it's simply becoming more expensive to maintain the effectiveness we've enjoyed.*

This focus on speed and execution has grown so bad that at a recent workshop that Joe and I were teaching, an attendee— a marketing director for a large food brand—came up to us and recounted the story of his latest job interview.

He said that he had met with the marketing team at another food brand to see if he was appropriate for a new digital marketing director position. In the interview, the team asked him what he might do in his first few weeks on the job. He proceeded to outline how he might work with the team to develop a new content strategy to apply to marketing, content marketing, and social media. The team cut him off and said, "What if we don't have time for that?" He asked, "You don't have time for strategy?" The team said, "No, we need to deliver ROI. We don't have time for analysis. We just need you to come in and start getting results with social posts and email. How would you do that?"

He didn't get the job.

What if We Actually Killed Marketing and Restructured It Completely?

What would happen if we completely flipped the idea of the marketing function on its head?

- What if instead of *starting* with trying to figure out the features and benefits of the products we offer for sale, we approached the whole structure and function of marketing by leading from our media strategy. What if we went from campaigns where we try to reach customers with frequency and persuade them to "buy now" to an editorial strategy approach that created valuable experiences for audiences that actually want to hear from us?

- What if instead of trying to figure out how our owned media can support our advertising campaigns, we started with how paid media advertising can support our owned media original content strategy?

- What if spending all our time trying to optimize digital advertising to make it ever cheaper, we ceded that creating original content requires different talent, is a more expensive endeavor, but can add more and different kinds of business value than simply clicks, conversions, and sales?

What if We Looked at Marketing as a Business Model Rather Than as a Functional Cost Center?

In *Experiences: The 7th Era of Marketing*, Carla and I told the story of Kathy Button Bell and her role as chief marketing officer for Emerson. She kicked off her position with a massive rebranding effort. Certainly that's not that different. But then as we note in the book, she spent the next 10 years instilling the editorial "story" of Emerson as the launching point for every other marketing and sales touchpoint. She instilled a culture of storytelling in the organization as a foundation on which every other effort would arise. In short, instead of trying to position marketing as the department that *described* the value of Emerson products and services, she created an entire strategy of one that *creates* value for customer audiences wherever they may be.

As we note in the book:

> Button Bell and her team have cultivated a brand story that resonates with businesses around the world and infiltrates every niche of the brand—from research and development to human resources and new business models. Emerson's "Consider It Solved" story centers on reducing complexity and how the company solves people's problems. Every story the company tells and every activity they take part in stems from the "Consider It Solved" story.

But what if we took it one step further? What if we not only killed the marketing we know today as the department that maximizes reach and frequency of our message and simply describes the value of our product and service, but transformed some part of our marketing into a revenue center? What if we could create a marketing function that creates so much value for audiences and consumers that it actually begins to pay for itself? What if it actually paid for itself so much that it started to actually make more money than it spent?

What if Marketers Did Marketing at a Profit?

One of the stories that you'll hear more about in the pages that follow focuses on Victor Gao. The company he works for, Arrow Electronics, is number 119 on the Fortune 500, has more than $24 billion in annual revenue, and has been a leader in the industry for more than 80 years.

Over the last two years, Arrow Electronics has watched as electronics publications that it heavily advertises in struggle. And for the company's customers, electrical engineers, not only were these publications how they kept up with what was going on in the industry—they were how kids became enamored and inspired to become electrical engineers. These publications are, quite literally, the lifeline for increasing the knowledge and population size of the Arrow Electronics customer base.

And so the concern for their health was real. As Victor said when we interviewed him, "Many of these niche publications are buried in the belly of much larger media conglomerates." And publishing about electronics may not be their highest priority.

Arrow has seized this opportunity. The company saw the tremendous need to serve engineers. Where the big media conglomerates couldn't afford to digitize small-circulation print magazines, Arrow could. Where the success of niche-oriented publications weren't in the interest of the media parent companies, it was directly linked to Arrow's success.

Over the last two years, Arrow Electronics has established itself as the largest media company in electronics. In February of 2015, Arrow purchased 16 engineering websites, e-newsletters, inventory access tools, and databases from Hearst's United Technical Publications. One year later, the company acquired the entire electronics media portfolio of UBM, including the brands EE Times, EDN, SEM, Embedded, EBN, TechOnline, and DataSheets.com for $23.5 million.

The new content and marketing portfolio for Arrow Electronics sells advertising to competitors and partners, holds events—and develops educational content for electronics professionals. (Joe will go into more detail on Arrow's revenue model in Chapter 3.) And the effort is 100 percent on developing value for the consumer. As Gao said to us, "I can tell you that we're highly profitable. But we reinvest that money into the editorial coverage and into the product experience."

Arrow is playing the long game here. By transforming a part of its marketing into an editorially led strategy, it is doing more than just focusing on describing the value of Arrow's products. Gao said it best in our interview:

> We think about the brightest, most talented kids. When we think about who we're competing with there—it's not our competitors. We compete with management consulting, or fashion, or other career choices these kids may have. So, the more of those bright young kids that we can attract to the electronics industry, at some point they will become customers to our industry. And we are supremely confident in our ability to grab our fair share of the market—as long as it keeps growing. So, our job, with this part of our marketing—is to make sure that the underlying market keeps growing. And we can make money doing exactly that.

Arrow Electronics and Victor Gao are part of the early group of innovators who are completely redefining how marketing markets. As I said earlier, this isn't about changing what Peter Drucker said was the business's main goal: "to create and keep a customer." It is, quite ironically, staying more true to exactly what Drucker meant when he said that "marketing and innovation produce results" than to much of what we do as marketers today.

Killing the marketing we know and replacing it with something entirely new may, quite frankly, be the only way to save the practice that we so love.

If you're ready—then let's get to work.

Profitable Insights

- The purpose of marketing has not changed. It is still, as Peter Drucker said, "to create and keep a customer." However, let's take Drucker at his word: "create." Creating a customer is more than simply persuading someone who is interested in buying something. It is, literally, *creating* a customer—from nothing. Marketers make markets—and today our opportunity is to create an interested audience as our first step. Then, the job is to keep the people in that audience interested in our approach until, and after, they actually purchase something from us.

- Owned media has grown beyond a simple marketing tactic, or even a marketing strategy. It is now a strategic business activity that marketers happen to perform. In order to make it profitable, we must restructure the priorities of marketing accordingly.

- Successful businesses of the future will utilize their relationships with an audience to draw multiple lines of value, and lead with editorial strategies that feed more traditional marketing and advertising activities.

Profitable Resources

- *Wikipedia*, s.v. "Paul Virilio," accessed May 1, 2017, https://en.wikipedia.org/wiki/Paul_Virilio#cite_note-shipwreck-4.

- Pulizzi and Rose, *Managing Content Marketing* (2011).

Profitable Resources (continued)

- Adam Levy, "HBO Now's Subscriber Growth Is Accelerating," Fool.com, February 13, 2017, https://www.fool.com/investing/2017/02/13/hbo-now-subscriber-growth-is-accelerating.aspx.

- Trefis Team, "Netflix Subscriber Growth Continues Unabated as Margins Improve," Forbes.com, January 19, 2017, http://www.forbes.com/sites/greatspeculations/2017/01/19/netflix-subscriber-growth-continues-unabated-as-margins-improve/#40e797103437.

- Todd Spangler, "Netflix Targets 50% of Content to Be Original Programming, CFO Says," Variety.com, September 20, 2016, http://variety.com/2016/digital/news/netflix-50-percent-content-original-programming-cfo-1201865902/.

- Joseph Lichterman, "After Trump's Election News Organizations See a Bump in Subscriptions and Donations," NiemanLab.org, November 14, 2016, http://www.niemanlab.org/2016/11/after-trumps-election-news-organizations-see-a-bump-in-subscriptions-and-donations/.

- Adam Levy, "Amazon's Biggest Advantage Is in Original Content," Fool.com, March 19, 2016, https://www.fool.com/investing/general/2016/03/19/amazons-biggest-advantage-in-original-content.aspx.

- Philip H. Dougherty, "Advertising Print Production Costs Up by Less Than 2%," *New York Times*, February 2, 1983,

http://www.nytimes.com/1983/02/02/business/
advertising-print-production-costs-up-by-less-than-2.html.

■ Dana Severson, "The Average Cost of National Advertising
Campaigns," AZCentral.com, accessed May 1, 2017,
http://yourbusiness.azcentral.com/average-cost-national
-advertising-campaigns-26091.html.

■ Jason Lynch, "U.S. Adults Consume an Entire Hour
More of Media per Day Than They Did Just Last Year,"
AdWeek.com, June 27, 2016, http://www.adweek.com/
tv-video/us-adults-consume-entire-hour-more-media-day
-they-did-just-last-year-172218/.

■ "Facebook Has 50 Minutes of Your Time Each Day. It
Wants More," *New York Times*, May 1, 2017, https://
www.nytimes.com/2016/05/06/business/facebook-bends
-the-rules-of-audience-engagement-to-its-advantage.html.

■ Joe Lazauskas, "'We Believe in Stories': GE Reports' Tomas
Kellner Reveals How He Built the World's Best Brand
Mag," Contently.com, February 11, 2015, https://con-
tently.com/strategist/2015/02/11/we-believe-in
-stories-ge-reports-tomas-kellner-reveals-how-he-built
-the-worlds-best-brand-mag/.

■ Liz Bedor, "Why Amex OPEN Forum Is Still the Gold
Standard for Content Marketing," Lizbedor.com, accessed
May 1, 2017, https://lizbedor.com/2015/08/11/american
-express-open-forum-content-marketing/.

■ Pulizzi and Barrett, *Get Content, Get Customers* (2009).

■ Victor Gao, interview by Claire McDermott, January 2017.

2

Return on Audience

**BY
ROBERT
ROSE**

That was the moment I gave up on decision analysis. No one ever made a decision because of a number. They need a story.

—Daniel Kahneman

You may hate gravity, but gravity does not care.

—Clayton Christensen

If, indeed, we are going to kill marketing, we should know what it is we are killing, and what we're replacing it with.

So, let's start with what we're killing. What is marketing?

You might be surprised at just how modern the word *marketing* is. Now, there is certainly debate about how long the word itself has been around. Some scholars trace it all the way back to the Dutch in the 1600s.

But then let me introduce you to Maria Parloa—or Miss Parloa, as she more normally went by (Figure 2.1). Maria Parloa was arguably America's first celebrity chef. Born in Massachusetts

Figure 2.1	Maria Parloa, America's first celebrity chef

in 1843, Maria was orphaned early in life. But at some point during her young childhood, she learned to cook. As she wrote in her first book, *The Appledore Cook Book*, "*having had years of experience as a cook in private families and hotels, I know the wants of the masses, and feel competent to supply them.*"

Maria opened her first of many cooking schools in October of 1877 in Boston, and within 10 years she became one of the most famous cooking instructors of her day. She was almost certainly one of the first people to ever make money by simply endorsing food products.

However, it's not for her cooking celebrity that we tell this story—it's for her fourth book, *Miss Parloa's New Cook Book: A Guide to Marketing and Cooking*, first published in 1881. It is in the title of this book that the word *marketing* appeared for the first (or certainly one of the first) times in American history.

Now, of course, what Miss Parloa meant by *marketing* would hardly match our current definition of it. For Miss Parloa, *marketing* was a verb that defined the activity of going to the market and strategically navigating your way through it. As Miss Parloa wrote in the introduction to her book:

> Many think the market not a pleasant or proper place for ladies. The idea is erroneous. My experience has been that there are as many gentlemen among marketmen as are to be found engaged in any other business. One should have a regular place at which to trade, as time is saved and disappointment obviated. If not a judge of meat, it is advisable, when purchasing, to tell the dealer so, and rely upon him to do well by you. If a housekeeper makes a practice of going to the market herself, she is able to supply her table with a better variety than she is by ordering at the door, or by note.

And while it was certainly not the "marketing" we would think of today—Miss Parloa's ardent case that "marketmen" were okay to be "trusted," would portend some of the very trust that the practice has today.

THE MARKETING "PROBLEM"

Around the turn of the century when Miss Parloa was enjoying her biggest celebrity, "marketing" was a mostly unknown practice among those that were looking to sell their product. But those who did business with those that were commonly called "middle men" described it as the marketing "problem." Most prominent was the disconnect between farmers who wanted to optimize where their crops could be sold and the middle men who promised they could help do exactly that. As the book *Marketing: A Critical Textbook* put it in 2011:

> While such criticism of the efficiency of the marketing system continues, theoretically, this topic raised an important question about marketing—were there any elements in distribution channels, for example, that were not adding some form of utility?

In other words, business owners were asking what the tangible value was in inserting a middle man between the production of a product or service and his promise to more quickly get that product into the hands of a consumer.

So we see that 130 years after Miss Parloa published her book, CEOs were still trying to figure out what the heck marketers did that added any value at all. It's nice to know how far we've come. Not.

MEASURING THE INVESTMENT IN MARKETING

Indeed, the challenge of measuring the value of marketing is certainly not new. It's not as if we somehow lost some capacity that we had in the 1910s or 1930s or 1960s. Marketers have been discussing the struggle of measuring performance for as long as marketing has been around. John Wannamaker famously said in the late 1800s, "*I know half my advertising is wasted; the trouble is I don't know which half.*"

Consider the very last line from a 1964 article "The Concept of the Marketing Mix," by Neil Borden, then professor emeritus of marketing and advertising at Harvard Business School. He was discussing the highly desired, but still unfulfilled, quest for the "science of marketing" and concluded with:

> We hope for a gradual formulation of clearly defined and helpful marketing laws. Until then, and even then, marketing and the building of marketing mixes will largely lie in the realm of art.

Joe and I very much appreciate the *"even then"* part of that last sentence. We suspect Professor Borden knew that looking for "laws" would be a frustrating journey.

Skip ahead 24 years and consider a comment in the book *Marketing Performance Assessment* from 1988. In the opening chapter, "The Philosopher's Stone," the authors say:

> The assessment of marketing performance, often called marketing productivity analysis, remains a seductive but elusive concept for scholars and practitioners alike. It is elusive because for as long as marketers have practiced their craft they have looked unsuccessfully for clear, present, and reliable signals of performance by which marketing merit could be judged.

In short, throughout the last 100 years, we have felt a compelling need to tilt the scales from art toward science; we have held up business laws that, if obeyed, would guarantee success. We really want the algorithm. And the truth is, we never get there.

And in varying degrees over the last century, this push toward the "laws" and "science" of marketing has been reduced to three little letters: ROI. From the *Mad Men* era forward, we've explored ways to figure out the right formula to extract a financial return from the investment of marketing. Whether called simple ROI (return on investment), or ROMI (return on marketing investment), or even ROC (return on customer—thank you Dr. Martha Rogers and Don Peppers), the goal has been the same: maximize the profitable return on the investment of the marketing effort.

But there's a problem.

We have always been terrible at doing it.

THE NEW MARKETING PROBLEM 2017

Here's a true story. Last year, Joe and I worked with a business-to-business manufacturing company. It sells products in industrial high-volume versions (pallets on a truck) to big companies, as well as through pick, pack, and ship methods through e-commerce to smaller companies and even individuals.

In 2015, this company had an incredible year. It grew sales by 650 percent. It happened to be the first year that the leaders hired a marketing director and invested in the practice. So, at the end of that year, they decided to do a review—a complete analysis of every single one of their marketing campaigns—and see which combination of efforts contributed the best to that growth number. What they found astounded them.

When they went back and looked at every marketing campaign that they ran in the previous 12 months, without fail every single one of them, on their own, would be considered a failure. Each one provided a flat return or no return at all.

They examined PPC (pay-per-click) search advertising. Overall, it was a cost. The cost of keywords and retargeting couldn't really be attributed to a number of customers or revenue that drove a profitable result. Their event marketing was *very* expensive, and—while it could be credited for a few customers buying product—it was pretty much a break-even effort. And when they added in the travel costs and time of their people, event marketing itself went into the red.

Advertising was incredibly hard to track for this company. But the marketing people tried to provide attribution to advertising in increased traffic and tracked web sales from those traffic sources. This was a dismal failure. Very few who came to the e-commerce site through banner ads ended up purchasing while they were there.

The company looked at lead nurturing—and the more enterprise customers. But they found that there was no one campaign that drove a preponderance of leads. The costs were about the same.

Over and over, each marketing campaign on its own—at best—broke even. And at worst, lost money. But the pure and simple fact was: the company grew by 650 percent. How could this be?

So, the CFO of the company took another approach. He asked each department—marketing, inside sales, PR, and the e-commerce team—to look at all its available analytics and provide an analysis of how it contributed to the 650 percent growth. Each did.

The result of this exercise was even more baffling. After each department reported its successful efforts, the CFO tabulated them all together, and he did find claims that totaled 650 percent growth. In fact, he found that if he were to believe all of the individual departments, the company should have actually grown by 1,850 percent. That's right—they all believed that their efforts alone contributed to all the growth.

As he said to us in an interview, "When we looked at all the campaigns individually—everything failed. But when we had each department look at their efforts—we should have grown at almost 2,000 percent." We asked, "So, what do you think happened?" The

CFO said, "Well, I guess *marketing* happened. So now we look at the investment in marketing as a whole, and not the individual campaigns."

This story is, broadly speaking, why ROI is the wrong kind of metric to use for whether marketing is worth doing. The simple fact is this: **Marketing, as we know it, isn't an investment. It's currently a cost that sometimes, in total, provides benefits for the money spent.**

Ask yourself: Are you trying to understand if the effort *did* work or whether it *will* work? If the former, you must capture measurements that quantify whether you met your goal. But let's be clear; goals such as incremental sales revenue, cost per lead generated, cost per sale generated, and cost of a new customer are *not* returns on an investment, nor are they even really goals. These are accountability metrics *toward* a particular business goal such as higher revenue or decreased costs.

Thinking of these things as return on investment is a bit like thinking of how your "investment" in gasoline produces a return on your job. Gasoline, like many marketing tactics, is ultimately a cost, not an investment; its fluctuating price and, literally, usage based on how you drive that week have no bearing on how it may boost your job performance in the short term. And it, inherently, can only generate a short-term benefit—getting you to work faster than walking.

Each marketing campaign is a new tank of gas, a project executed in a short time frame that we evaluate as a one-time return on that effort. Stack enough of those together, and you can create a smart strategy—and theoretically a return on your overall investment in the practice of marketing. Like the CFO said: we invest in "marketing," not individual campaigns.

Campaign-focused marketing is a recognized cost of improving the short-term performance of our business. We could talk much more about this point, but for now let's move to the second question we need to ask: *Will it work?*

This question is more common for those focused on redefining marketing because whatever innovative, or new, thing we want to do is usually something that hasn't been done before. Today, when ROI comes up, it's usually because marketers are being asked to make a case for the success of something that's never been done before.

Ironically, this brings us right back to the first problem. Our only frame of reference to make that case is our past performance (as Joe outlined in the Introduction). This is a catch-22. In short, you're being asked to "*tell me what you already know*" in order to prove "*how certain you are about this new thing you want to do.*" **In short: tell me how confident you are about the future of your job by examining historical fuel prices for your car.**

Yeah, it's a guess.

But here's the larger problem with ROI in marketing. It encourages us to underperform.

Both Joe and I have worked with a few companies where ROI as a percentage is the primary metric that determines whether that marketer is successful or not. In other words, these managers don't look at the success of the company; they examine whether—as a percentage—they are delivering a higher return based on whatever budget they are provided. One of these companies has slowly degraded its marketing budget to under 1.5 percent of revenue. It is flailing in the marketplace, suffering from slow growth—but delivering a high ROI on its marketing investment. What happened?

If marketing's mandate is to maximize ROI, you have every incentive to never do anything new at all. Look at it this way. Let's pretend your mandate is to maximize marketing's ROI percentage. If I spend $200 in marketing to get to $250 in revenue—then technically my ROI is 25 percent. But if I spend $0 and make

$100—my ROI is 100 percent (or really infinite). To maximize my marketing ROI percentage, it's actually smarter for me to spend *no* money and hope for one sale than to spend some money and hope for many sales.

This is an extreme example, but it holds true over time. As you increase market penetration, the rate at which you win new customers naturally slows. It must. Yet because you're now spending a portion of your marketing budget on return sales, your marketing ROI, as a percentage, will eventually decrease. That's why applying ROI to a process that is ultimately a cost, not an increasingly valuable long-term asset, can be treacherous at best.

Now we want to be clear—we're not suggesting that marketing is completely immeasurable. Certainly there are great examples of companies that have begun to solve the attribution challenge. And this is not necessarily a book about marketing measurement. However, one of the biggest reasons we see companies balking at getting into new models is because of the "measurability challenge." So . . .

WHAT IF THERE WERE A BETTER WAY?

We have to ask ourselves if the marketing we are doing today can withstand the realities of the future. Technology's inevitable advance is promising a world in which small chores such as deciding which razor to purchase, or which mattress to choose, or which condiments and salad dressings are the best will come via subscription. Today, with technology such as Amazon's Dash Button, we can literally press an Internet-connected big red button to automatically reorder our home's staples. Why ever consider another brand again?

As we evolve into a world driven by algorithms, chatbots, and automation, the need to differentiate becomes one of holistic experience, rather than differentiated features or brand attributes. As the great Don Schultz, professor emeritus at Northwestern, says, everything we do as an organization can be copied, *except* for how we communicate.

In fact, research just published by consulting group McKinsey has found that being in the initial consideration set of brands may be the largest component to growing share of market. As McKinsey states in its research:

> Investing too much of your marketing dollars in loyalty is risky when today's shop-around environment means it's easy to lose consumers faster than you add new ones. Instead, companies that hope to move the growth needle need more focus on innovative programs for the 87 percent of consumers out there who are likely to look beyond their current brand.

Today, we not only have an opportunity to look to a better method of measuring our efforts across creating business value through marketing; we have an opportunity to completely redefine the entire practice. The key is looking to the investment we are making as one that is not focused on the immediate return of transactional clicks, visits, paths, time on site, or even purchases, but rather the accumulation of attention and access to an audience we can monetize over time.

This is not just a marketing tactics transformation—this is a business transformation. This is looking at marketing as a business model—a profitable investment that is meant to provide access, and accumulation of attention and loyalty from a true investment: an audience.

We can ask these questions:

■ How much more valuable is Red Bull as a company because it has a marketing strategy that draws revenue and positions its brand as a company that can sell any kind of product that its audience wants. Because Red Bull has accumulated a loyal audience, it is no longer limited to selling an energy drink. Its business is in creating an audience—and then selling the individuals in the audience products that meet their needs.

- How much more valuable is Arrow Electronics as a company because it has 51 digital magazines, websites, and an audience that is loyal to that content? It is subsidizing the growth of its TAM (total addressable market) and educating an entire industry. Arrow Electronics is using a new marketing approach as an insurance policy. They are ensuring that the community of educated, engaged, electrical engineers will continue to grow, and will ultimately find Arrow's offerings the best for their needs.

- How much more valuable is Lego the media company, rather than Lego the manufacturing company? Its investment in audiences including feature films, television, magazines, and digital platforms have made it more content-centric than toy-centric. As Conny Klacher, Lego's vice president of marketing and consumer experiences, said: "*We used to be a toy manufacturer. Now we're turning more and more into a media company to tell our story about these bricks.*"

The answer to how much more valuable is, for the moment, elusive—though we would note that Red Bull, as a private company, has an estimated brand value of $7.9 billion. Lego, also a private company, said that 2015 was its best year ever with growth of more than 25 percent. And over the last five years, Arrow Electronics' stock price has grown 43 percent.

Certainly, there's a "causation or correlation" challenge there. But there is one thing that these companies have in common. They have significant investment in a process associated with marketing that delivers value through operating as a media company and creating direct relationships with addressable audiences.

RETURN ON AUDIENCE

There are really only two core metrics we care about as a business—increasing revenue and decreasing costs (Figure 2.2). We can further break these two broad categories out into what we call our Four "C" Investment Goals of Value for investing in audience: Competency, Campaign, Customer, and Cash. And each of the Four Cs can themselves be broken out into Win, Grow, Keep, Direct subcategories, with different types of objectives that may be appropriate for different kinds of companies.

We'll cover each of the Four Cs individually in the following sections of this chapter.

Figure 2.2	Revenue versus savings

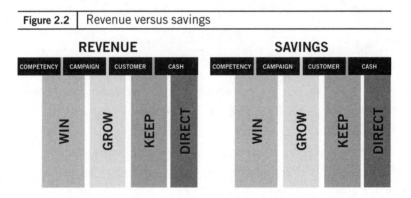

Competency—Making a Smarter Company

One of the critical things to understand about the investment in an audience is that it is made up of people who *want to hear* from the brand—continually. Investing in the data that an audience will provide is not simply aggregating past shopping data or surveilling what "buyers" do on our digital properties. Rather, this data is given to us willingly, rather than gathered. These are people who are willingly sharing their personal data, interacting with our tools, and giving us permission to converse with them because we are delivering value through the content-driven experience.

This value exchange means that the data gleaned from these audiences can be very valuable to other parts of our organization.

One example of this is Schneider Electric, a global company that specializes in energy management and automation solutions. With more than $25 billion in revenue, it has a multitude of marketing and sales efforts across the world. Susan Hartman is the global program manager for Energy University, Schneider Electric's free e-learning resource. The platform delivers courses in 12 languages and has been endorsed by more than a dozen professional and trade organizations for continuing education credits. Over the last few years more than 180,000 learners have gone through the university. When Susan sat down with us to talk about her company's success, she mentioned this idea of using the data to understand Schneider's audience:

> We do end up understanding our audience better because of the data we collect. When you register into Energy University, you put in a certain amount of data about yourself. This is where it differs than just a normal marketing platform, because it's a learning system, and so the data is more complete. Then, we watch the trend of what courses you're taking, what you're interested in, and what you respond back to us about wanting more of. We utilize that data to help us understand more about who you are, and what products you may ultimately be looking to buy.

There are other examples of this as well. Consider Johnson & Johnson and its online property BabyCenter.com. The global pharmaceutical company acquired BabyCenter.com in March of 2001, and it has operated the platform as a separate division ever since. The site sells advertising and sponsorships, and according to the research company Quantcast, it reaches more than 23 million people every month.

Now why would J&J operate a completely independent website that has nothing to do with its core business of selling products? For J&J, it seems to be all about the data. According to an interview with Christina Hoff, Johnson & Johnson's manager of global strategic insights, the value is in "combining a research panel of 50,000 consumers with the insights it gains from the sentiments shared by mothers worldwide on BabyCenter.com."

As she explained to *Adweek* in 2014: "We can tell what a mom is going to do before she does [it] based on what she is searching for." The company knows, for example, that mothers plan for their baby's first birthday when the child is 10 months old. Or when brand managers for J&J products such as Tylenol or Motrin want to know whether their ad headline should read "sleep through the night," "sleep tonight," or "sleep overnight," the company can tell which one of those should be the most resonant with mothers based on BabyCenter posts.

Whether it's adding new revenue-generating platforms such as J&J's BabyCenter.com or a cost-saving marketing platform such as Schneider's Energy University—the value is clear. *If* we can begin to gather more valuable data from our audience, we can become a more competent company—and enable much better business decisions across the sales and marketing spectrum.

Campaign Value—Supporting Transactional, Promotional Efforts

As we explained earlier in the chapter, the main driver of value over the last three decades has been to optimize the "marketing mix"—our effort to reach audiences through rented platforms that can drive a favorable action. Put more simply, we spend money on campaigns that attempt to optimize how many eyeballs we can get our message in front of. And then we measure ourselves by the ratio of that cost to how many of those people actually do what we want them to do. One of the earliest benefits of the media marketing model and the aggregation of an audience is to create an opportunity to make these campaigns more effective.

Most of the books and case studies in content marketing have focused here. In Joe's book *Epic Content Marketing*, Joe talked about Indium, a company that refines, produces, supplies, and fabricates Indium chemicals for the global electronics semiconductor, solar, thin-film, and thermal management markets. In case you didn't catch that—Indium is about as conservative and niche a business as you will find in the world today. But as Joe described in his book:

> Seventeen engineers from materials supplier Indium have discovered content gold with their From One Engineer to Another blog. Through it, they produce valuable content, videos, and answer questions about a variety of engineering topics (for example, how to set up and operate the Indium sulfamate plating bath). Even if you don't know what that means, you can appreciate what they are striving for: to bring ideas to life through interactive conversations. According to Indium's marketing director, they've seen a 600 percent jump in leads since the launch.

Marketing thought leader and international speaker Andrew Davis calls the audience a "pre-customer database." We love that term—as it illuminates a core truth. An audience that you are delivering value to today may not be in the market for your product or service. But the audience members will be more than happy to tell you when they *are* in the market for your product or service, and you will be top of mind when they are. And isn't that exactly the goal of our continual focus on reach and frequency in today's campaign-oriented strategy? We want to be top of mind when our customer is ready to purchase, and thus we try to continually bombard the media with our message, to make sure that we're hitting that consumer just in case *now* is the time. We are, quite literally, like the kid in the back seat of the car asking, "Are we there yet, are we there yet, are we there yet?" Instead, using an aggregated audience as our "pre-customer database," we can more effectively hold people's attention over time—have them provide the other lines of value until they are ready to purchase.

And that brings us to the third core value from this new approach to marketing.

Customer Value—Creating a More Valuable Customer

In the early days of custom publishing—one of the original terms for content marketing—content created by brands was almost exclusively focused on loyalty. "House organs"—or employee magazines—were created to make those who worked for the company feel a sense of belonging to the enterprise, and customer loyalty magazines were created to make customers feel better about their purchase. Today, these kinds of experiences are one of the first that are actually enjoying this new sense of "marketing at a profit."

Customer events, content-driven apps, and even print magazines are being utilized not only to make customers feel better about their purchase, but to add separate, discrete value to their purchases from the brand.

Consider investment company TD Ameritrade, which focuses on clients who are interested in trading stocks. Once these customers are acquired, the company provides them with access to its thinkorswim.com community—and specifically signs them up for *thinkMoney* magazine—a print and digital magazine. The goal of this content-driven experience is to continually engage traders (after they become customers) and empower them with the right tools, tips, research, and capabilities for them to trade more effectively. They've learned that subscribers to the magazine trade five times more than nonsubscribers. That's something that will never be delivered with a paid advertisement. It's a valuable experience, separate from the product, that creates a more engaged and frequent customer.

Once leads and prospects become customers, they are prime to become an audience that the company can engage and in whom it can create a larger sense of brand loyalty.

Consider Nike. The company began developing branded apps for mobile devices in 2006. Now, the company has multiple apps for mobile phones focused on helping runners and athletes in tracking progress. As magazine *Ad Age* recently reported:

> Collectively, these apps boast a user base of over 28 million people. That is 28 million people to which the brand has direct access. With this greater customer intimacy, Nike gains invaluable insights and information about its user base. With access to all this information, Nike could have used it to aggressively drive sales from the app, but instead has brilliantly created a real athlete community by means of its apps. Through this genuine community Nike has built from the ground up, it fosters intense brand loyalty which translates to revenue down the line.

That is the power of an aggregated audience, and it changes the remit of marketing considerably.

And this brings us to our fourth category for marketing value: Cash.

Cash—Generating Direct Revenue from the Marketing Program

This value is new, and it is squarely where our book is focused. Direct revenue is certainly the most unorthodox of the different kinds of value that an audience can provide with marketing as a business model.

Leading companies are generating direct revenue from their audiences. And they are diversifying their business, generating a higher margin and/or mitigating costs of other marketing activities with this strategy. They are, when combined with the savings attributed to other values, marketing at a *profit*.

As we've mentioned a few times in this book, there may be no more explicit example of this model than Red Bull. To quote from the Introduction:

> Today, Red Bull Media House is one of the world's most successful media companies. What started as a simple magazine has evolved into TV series, documentaries, world-class events, a music studio, and merchandising, and Red Bull even licenses its content to traditional media companies like the *New York Times*.

Or consider Salesforce.com. In 2003 1,000 Salesforce.com customers squeezed into the Westin hotel in San Francisco to see the newest updates from the software provider. In 2016, the event has grown to 170,000 people and is the largest software event on the planet. That's right—the biggest software education event in the world is not hosted by a media company—it is hosted by a software company. Now, the attendee list price was $1,799 per person. Let's assume that 30 percent of the attendees paid that. That would be more than $91 million in revenue from this customer event. And that doesn't take into account all the sponsorships that Salesforce.com also sells. A platinum sponsorship for the event goes for more than $1 million each. While Salesforce.com doesn't separate out the revenue from this event, I think it's safe to assume that the company makes money at it.

THE NEW MARKETING MANTRA

At the beginning of this book, Joe discussed Philip Kotler's concept that he called the "new marketing mantra." He said it was CCDVTP:

> Create, Communicate, and Deliver Value
> to a Target market at a Profit.

In our view, this is a perfect foundation for a completely new approach to marketing. Marketing is no longer simply the department or team that describes the value of the product or service we put into the marketplace. Marketing must be led, strategically, by a core story—an editorial value that places the creation of differentiating value for customers through content-driven experiences. Marketing must communicate this value not only to prospective customers, but throughout the organization. The media strategy *leads* the product marketing features and benefits, and it delivers value across the Four Cs of Competency, Campaign, Consumer, and Cash to a target. And perhaps most of all, it does so as a profit-oriented venture—rather than as a cost-based structure. It may not be the highest margin of the business, and it may purposely run at a flat, or even slightly loss-based, cost structure.

We must kill the marketing that makes its living from accessing audiences for short bursts of time so that they might buy our product.

We must rebirth a new marketing that makes its living from building audiences for long periods of time, so that we might hold their attention through experiences that place us squarely in the initial consideration set when they are looking for a solution.

This is the marketing of the future. It is achieving a long-term return on the *one* asset that will save our business: an audience.

Profitable Insights

- Measuring the practice of marketing has not gotten any easier or better since the origin of the practice. More data has not enabled us to be any more accurate with our measurement. But looking at measurement as a means of monitoring our investment in marketing as a business model is achievable.

- Audiences can provide for multiple lines of value. They provide campaign value, enabling smarter marketing and advertising. They provide for competency value, enabling the acquisition of data to make us a smarter business. They provide customer value, helping us develop more loyal customers who will advocate for our brand. And audience can provide cash value, enabling us to make marketing a profitable venture.

Profitable Resources

- *Wikipedia*, s.v. "Maria Parloa," accessed May 1, 2017, https://en.wikipedia.org/wiki/Maria_Parloa.

- Jack, Fitchett, Higgins, Lim, and Ellis, *Marketing: A Critical Textbook* (2011).

Profitable Resources *(continued)*

- Neil Borden, "The Concept of the Marketing Mix," accessed on Slideshare.net on May 1, 2017, https://www.slideshare.net/wgabriel/neil-borden-heconceptofthemarketingmixblogwgabriel.

- David Court, Dave Elzinga, Bo Finneman, and Jesko Perrey, "The New Battleground for Marketing-Led Growth," *McKinsey Quarterly*, February 2017, Mckinsey.com, http://www.mckinsey.com/business-functions/marketing-and-sales/our-insights/the-new-battleground-for-marketing-led-growth.

- John Kell, "Lego Says 2015 Was Its 'Best Year Ever,' with Huge Sales Jump," Fortune.com, March 1, 2016, http://fortune.com/2016/03/01/lego-sales-toys-2015/.

- Susan Hartman from Schneider Electric, interview by Claire McDermott, January 2017.

- Christopher Heine, "Why Johnson & Johnson Treasures BabyCenter's Data," Adweek.com, April 2, 2014, http://www.adweek.com/digital/why-johnson-johson-treasures-babycenters-data-156720/.

- Joe Pulizzi, *Epic Content Marketing: How to Tell a Different Story, Break Through the Clutter, and Win More Customers by Marketing Less* (McGraw-Hill Education, 2014), 300.

- Richard Beeson, "Content Marketing Strategy," Agorapulse.com, May 27, 2014, http://www.agorapulse.com/blog/content-marketing-strategy-joe-pulizzi.

3

Media Marketing

BY
JOE
PULIZZI

The business model of racing is not a pretty one.

—Jeff Gordon

*My model for business is The Beatles: They were four guys
that kept each other's negative tendencies in check;
they balanced each other. And the total was greater than
the sum of the parts.*

—Steve Jobs

Earlier this year I took a much needed "vitamin D" vacation to Florida with my family (we live in Cleveland, Ohio).

After taking down one science fiction book (it was *Ready Player One* by Ernest Cline—a must-read for any science fiction or video game lover), my wife threw me the latest issue of *Cosmopolitan* magazine.

That's right . . . I was reading *Cosmo* (don't judge).

According to its media kit, *Cosmopolitan* magazine reaches a monthly audience of over 14 million women via its print magazine and over 50 million including digital channels. About 60 percent of the folks in its audience read at least three out of every four issues, and when they do, it's for an average of 75 minutes.

Seventy-five minutes. How's that for engagement?

Cosmo's stated mission is:

> to empower young women to own who they are and be who they want to be, and we're focused on propelling her into her fun, fearless future. No excuses, no bull@#*%, no regrets.

Let's take a minute to compare that to one of the largest companies in the world, Exxon Mobil, which states its mission as:

> Exxon Mobil Corporation is committed to being the world's premier petroleum and petrochemical company. To that end, we must continuously achieve superior financial and operating results while adhering to high ethical standards.

Notice the difference? (Besides the fun.)

THE CONTENT BUSINESS MODEL

Cosmo is completely focused on the audience. There isn't one word about what *Cosmo* sells to make a profit. Exxon, on the other hand, has a clear mission around what it sells. Oil . . . and lots of it. Good for Exxon.

Cosmo has made content its business model (as Robert details in Chapter 1).

*It is the strategic use of content that will not only build audiences and drive the creation and retention of customers; it can do so **at a profit**.*

Sounds like a media company, right? It should.

While traditionally *Cosmo*'s go-to revenue strategy revolves around selling advertising, Cosmo has a number of flexible options to make money from its content.

Cosmo's model looks something akin to this:

Create a loyal audience. Once we learn the deep-rooted needs of that audience, and we deliver value to the audience consistently, and the audience (reader) becomes a fan (subscriber), we monetize that relationship in multiple ways.

And *Cosmo* does, from books to beauty packages to native advertising to syndicated content to promotions (we'll go through more of this in the next chapter). If *Cosmo* leaders are even half-innovative, they'll see how many products they could sell directly to their readers (instead of mostly just selling access to advertisers). When that happens, watch out!

With Exxon, it's very challenging for a marketing professional to leverage content with a mission that revolves around the product (and not the customer). That's where, to Robert's examples in Chapter 1, content is a time-based tactic that should, if executed correctly, lead to more interest in the product.

MEDIA OR PRODUCT BRAND?

Exxon is one of the largest, most valuable companies in the world. It's leveraged every bit of traditional marketing and a traditional business model and has come up roses. But if Exxon wants to grow substantially bigger and become a growth company (if that's even possible), it needs to kill the model.

Now you may be wondering to yourself, "But Joe, *Cosmopolitan* is a media company, and Exxon sells a product. Of course the models should be different."

Should they?

Dennis Publishing is one of the largest independently owned media companies in the United Kingdom. Its big titles include *Men's Fitness* and *The Week*, but it also holds large content platforms in the automotive sector, including brands like *Car Buyer* and *Auto Express*.

Over the last 10 years, most media companies have struggled to grow significantly as print advertising continues to die a slow death. But this hasn't affected Dennis. According to *The Guardian*, Dennis Publishing has increased revenue from £59m in 2009 to £93m in 2016. How, you ask?

In November of 2014, Dennis acquired the online car dealer BuyaCar, which now generates 16 percent of Dennis's total revenue. That's correct. This little media company sells over 200 cars per day. Dennis had the audience (interested car buyers) and formed a loyal relationship with that audience over time. In hindsight, it was a no-brainer move for Dennis to buy an online car dealer or e-commerce company, and yet very few media companies see this as a possibility (for now).

So, is Dennis a media company or a brand that sells products and services? How about Red Bull or J&J?

Hollywood celebrity Gwyneth Paltrow launched Goop.com in 2008. Originally conceived as a weekly e-newsletter on travel recommendations and shopping tips, Goop quickly attracted over one million e-mail subscribers. Once Goop developed a committed, loyal audience, it started launching products, and in 2016, it announced and sold a full clothing line.

Is Goop a media company or a brand that, for now, sells fashionable clothing? What might it sell five years from now?

Today, if you had to choose between creating an audience and then directly selling to that audience, versus renting outside channels that you don't control and don't own, which would you choose? Of course, you'd go direct. It's an incredibly easy decision to make, and yet most companies have been choosing to rent (primarily) year after year. We keep sustaining, as Robert states, an "inefficient" system like it is the only game in town. We've been led to believe that our current marketing is the hand we've been dealt, and there's nothing more we can do.

> *This human understands enough to know when he's being messed with.*
>
> —From *Armada* by Ernest Cline

THE SAME MODEL

As Robert and I studied our research on large enterprise marketing departments as well as media companies over the past few years, both of us kept coming to the same exact conclusion:

The new media business model and the new marketing business model are exactly the same.

Here's an actual email conversation between Robert and me when we first starting putting together the ideas that turned into this book:

> *From: Joe Pulizzi*
> *Subject: Thoughts?*
> *Hey*
> *I know it's obvious, but it finally hit me that the new media model and the new marketing model are exactly the same.*
>
> *I just think that's so cool . . . is it obvious or is it really earth shattering?*

> *From: Robert Rose*
>
> *Subject: RE: Thoughts?*
>
> *No . . . It's EXACTLY the same . . . Remember when I was saying that I was CONVINCED that we were on to something huge here . . . That's the revelation . . . That's what has me so pumped about this . . .*
>
> *It's earth shattering I think . . . But maybe I'm just in this with you . . . Ha!*

What's the difference between Miami and Cleveland?
It's the same.

—LeBron James from the movie *Trainwreck*

Today, when you look at most media or product brands, you see a large difference. The *New York Times* versus Procter & Gamble. The *Economist* versus Intel. *IndustryWeek* magazine versus Lincoln Electric.

Most people have vastly different perceptions between what a media company does and what a product brand does. And today, for the most part, they are different. But as we move into 2020 and beyond, the business model differences between the two will dissolve away.

Media companies, like Dennis Publishing, will drive revenue from both traditional media products (subscriptions and advertising) and products and services (selling cars).

Product and service companies, like Arrow Electronics, will drive revenues from selling products and services (they sell industrial electronics equipment) as well as selling traditional media products (subscriptions and advertising).

When you build an audience, both sides of the revenue equation are possible. It's not just marketing . . . it's a business model.

Robert and I believe that those innovative companies that begin to implement this new content business model into the fabric of their current business model will be the ones that lead their industries in the future.

And Walt Disney knew this over 60 years ago.

DECONSTRUCTING DISNEY

Walt Disney's visual content model (go to https://hbr.org/2013/06/what-is-the-theory-of-your-firm if you'd like to view the image) from 1957 is one of my favorite documents (so much so that I have it hanging in my living room). The image shows Disney's collection of assets, from comic books to music to merchandise, which all build off each other. But central (actually placed in the center of the image) are animated and live-action films. That content is what Disney (the company) used to build a fan base (an audience). Then, that fan base, as the fans became more loyal through Disney's other content properties, began to spend money, specifically at Disneyland and through merchandising sales.

Todd Zenger from the University of Utah describes Disney's visual plan in these terms: "Disney sustains value-creating growth by developing an unrivaled capability in family-friendly animated (and live-action) films and then assembling other entertainment assets that both support and draw value from the characters and images in those films."

Long story short, Disney built an audience and then monetized that audience through traditional media and by selling products and services. Disney is one of the rare companies that was never a media company or a product brand—it's always been both . . . by design.

Content Marketing Institute (CMI), the company we launched in 2010 and then sold to UBM in 2016, follows the exact same model as Disney. So much so that we created a visual business model based on Disney's 1957 strategy (Figure 3.1).

Disney's core platform revolved around the theatrical films. That was Disney's first step to build a relationship with an audience. For CMI, the digital blog, where we deliver an original 1,500-word instructional story per day, is the core that generates the audience. From there, we make money from our fans in

Figure 3.1	CMI based its media business model directly on the Disney Productions visual model.

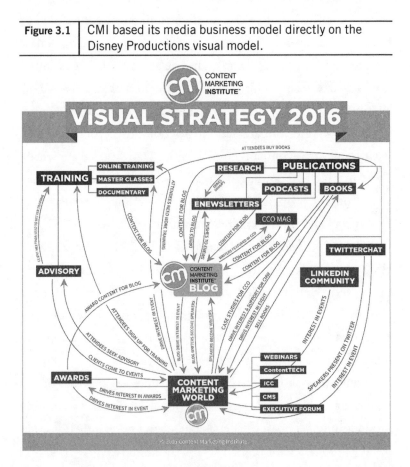

a number of ways, most specifically through our large in-person event Content Marketing World (just like Disney does through Disneyland and Disney World).

The interesting thing, as we'll talk at length about in the rest of this book, is the number of different ways a company can generate revenue once a loyal audience has been established through content value creation.

A BETTER MARKETING MODEL

As we've presented, marketing departments are now taking these formerly exclusive media business models and not only leveraging them for sales and cost savings goals, but doing so at a direct profit.

Let's take an in-depth look at three examples of this happening today: a business-to-consumer (B2C) company, a business-to-business (B2B) company, and a startup.

Under the Hood: Red Bull

> The Austrian energy drink brand cemented itself as the Coke of the shareable content era, willing to spend freely to produce content so good that it is indistinguishable from non-marketing content. Red Bull truly is a media company that happens to sell soft drinks.
>
> —Brian Morrissey, Digiday

I've stated that last line from the quote above in presentations hundreds of times over the past decade: "Red Bull is a media company that happens to sell soft drinks."

Red Bull is probably the most well-known example of marketing as a profit center. Through a variety of content efforts, Red Bull has secured one of the most loyal audiences on the planet. Red Bull Media House is the engine that makes this happen. You can put the media savvy of Red Bull Media House against any traditional media company in the world, from process through storytelling, and you'll have a hard time choosing which one is better.

When I first wrote about Red Bull Media House in my book *Epic Content Marketing* (2013), I believed that the content Red Bull created was just like any other content marketing program—the aim was to ultimately drive product sales. In this case, it would be to sell more cans of Red Bull. But as I discussed in the Introduction of this book, Red Bull Media House has one goal—to generate a direct profit from the created content. Sure, Red Bull management loves to see demand rise off the back of its content creation, but according to Red Bull editor Robert Sperl, Red Bull Media House is measured like any media company would be, off direct revenue and profit generation.

It does this through a number of initiatives. Here's a handful:

- **Print.** *The Red Bulletin*, a monthly print and digital magazine, is delivered to over two million subscribers around the world, published in ten countries and in five languages. *The Red Bulletin* is the company's flagship print magazine and is positioned as a global men's lifestyle magazine. Red Bull also has three other print magazines, including *Berg Welten*, an alpine adventure magazine, and *Terra Mater*, a nature and science magazine. Red Bull sells advertising and sponsorship within the magazine and also sells direct through subscriptions (just like any other traditional magazine).

- **Red Bull content pool.** The company licenses out thousands of videos, images, and music directly to media companies. Yes, that is correct: media companies pay Red Bull to license and purchase the rights to show Red Bull–branded content. Its premium content repository of digital imagery in the sports arena is second to maybe only Disney (ESPN).

- **Red Bull records.** With offices in Los Angeles and London, Red Bull Records signs performers, such as indie rock act Awolnation or the alternative band Twin Atlantic, to record deals that align with Red Bull's "Give You Wings" mentality. In addition, Red Bull Music Publishing backs aspiring composers and songwriters and then syndicates those songs as part of its content pool and in other Red Bull programs.

- **Speedweek.** Speedweek is the motor sports brand for Red Bull, focused on two-wheel and four-wheel racing. This mini-media company covers 70 different race classes and 360 championships. Speedweek sells digital advertising and mobile sponsorships to some of the leading companies in the world that are interested in reaching this particular fan base.

Add on Red Bull TV and Red Bull films and documentaries, as well as live programming covering extreme sports from around the world—Red Bull Media House "may" be second only to ESPN in consistent sports programming.

Under the Hood: Arrow Electronics

As Robert stated in Chapter 1, Arrow Electronics (NYSE: ARW), founded in 1935, is one of the largest companies in the world, generating over $24 billion in annual revenues. It is the world's largest distributor of electronic components, from semiconductors to circuit boards, and now services over 100,000 customers around the globe.

Arrow's media model came in two steps. According to Victor Gao, vice president and managing director, Arrow's digital presence was a federation of microsites and literally hundreds of domains in 2014. These sites had no integration with each other and, often, were devoid of Arrow branding. Simply put, the customer experience of those sites consistently ranked Arrow near the bottom in its industry. To remedy this, Arrow discontinued the microsite model and created one global experience at Arrow.com (and Chip1Stop, Arrow's Japanese brand). The sole goal of Arrow.com is to sell products and services.

Once the new site was complete, Arrow invested heavily in high-quality content answering the specific problems that electrical engineers had in and around the products Arrow sold. Each piece of content created was professionally written and edited and then reviewed by an expert Arrow electrical engineer. Less than a year after Arrow invested in original content and relaunched its site, it saw a 30-times increase in reader engagement (a combination of unique visitors and time spent). In the process, Arrow.com has become one of the most-trafficked sites in the industry.

That was step one. Step two revolved around research Arrow discovered in 2014 called the "Mind of the Engineer" from UBM (Figure 3.2). According to the research, the critical issue engineers were concerned about was keeping their engineering knowledge up-to-date. Then, the research listed 18 different ways in which engineers educated themselves on a daily basis. All but two of these ways were media, from blogs to podcasts to articles to seminars.

It was then that the Arrow management realized that the biggest opportunity for the company was to become the trusted

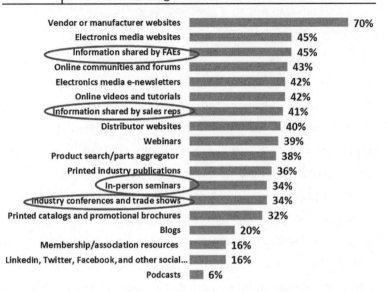

| Figure 3.2 | Electronics engineers almost exclusively get industry information through media. |

Vendor or manufacturer websites — 70%
Electronics media websites — 45%
Information shared by FAEs — 45%
Online communities and forums — 43%
Electronics media e-newsletters — 42%
Online videos and tutorials — 42%
Information shared by sales reps — 41%
Distributor websites — 40%
Webinars — 39%
Product search/parts aggregator — 38%
Printed industry publications — 36%
In-person seminars — 34%
Industry conferences and trade shows — 34%
Printed catalogs and promotional brochures — 32%
Blogs — 20%
Membership/association resources — 16%
LinkedIn, Twitter, Facebook, and other social... — 16%
Podcasts — 6%

resource for electronic engineers. Arrow made the decision to become the media.

Victor Gao stated:

Arrow didn't start a media company from scratch. We created the media portfolio with acquisition(s). . . . So if you were an electrical engineer, when you have an idea you probably started doing some research online, you look at some general technology articles. And then you move on to what's called a data sheet, which is a detailed description, often by the manufacturer of that component, of "here are all the different parametric parameters you need to think about." And there's a reference design, so it's a document that says, "Well, this component typically goes with these other components." And then you want to go onto a cloud based tool to run some simulations, then you actually want to order some prototypes . . . and do a bunch of tests and you iterate and eventually you get to the prototype of the entire product. And so, when we thought about [it] in terms of the media properties we have, we wanted to make sure that we can go along that journey for the engineer so we can . . . help them soup to nuts.

As of June 2017, Arrow owns 51 media properties in the electronics media space, becoming the largest media organization in the industry (in terms of unique visitors and time spent). The media properties are housed in a completely separate division of Arrow, called AspenCore, creating a very real firewall between the main company and the media properties (like editorial church/ state separation in traditional media companies).

Arrow analyzes AspenCore's performance through primary and secondary key performance indicators (KPIs). Primarily, AspenCore is judged on its financial performance, specifically, its profitability. According to Gao, AspenCore is highly profitable, with some advertisers and sponsors doubling their spend over the past two years. Secondary KPIs include reach (audience size), engagement (time spent), and social sharing.

But like Red Bull Media House, AspenCore is determined to be successful, or not, *exactly* like a media company would.

AspenCore drives revenues in the following ways:

- Web advertising on content brands like *EE Times*, *EEM*, and *Power Electronics News* including banners, button and pop-over ads, welcome and channel ads, and e-newsletter advertising.

- Sponsorships including webinars and webcasts, as well as sponsored and custom content offerings. (Arrow actually creates original content for outside companies.)

- Print advertising in publications such as *Electronic Products* magazine.

■ List rentals and data sales.

In addition, AspenCore offers discounted advertising and sponsorship to Arrow sub-brands in particular niches. This does two things for the brands: first, they are able to get direct reach and influence at a significant cost reduction over normal advertising; and second, the Arrow brands can get first-party data to educate them on what readers are interested in, and what they are not. This is very similar to what Kraft Foods has done for years with its *Food and Family* content brand. Kraft uses this type of first-party data as a form of research and development, and it helps the company determine what new products may be worthy of consideration based on the needs and pain points of the audience (what content the audience engages with, and doesn't, on Kraft's owned properties).

Under the Hood: Terminus

Red Bull and Arrow are two of the largest companies in the world. Once they received corporate approval to develop a media arm, both had the resources to invest heavily in the businesses from the very beginning.

But what if you don't have a significant budget? What if you are a startup? Is this "marketing and media company" thing just for large brands?

Terminus is a small startup from Atlanta, Georgia, that sells account-based marketing (ABM) software. Its software is specific to B2B marketing professionals that need to build relationships with 10, 15, or 20 different people at the same company in order to sell their product. Terminus's software helps to make sense of this process.

Sangram Vajre, cofounder and chief marketing officer at Terminus, came up with an idea called "Flip My Funnel," which he started to blog about consistently on LinkedIn's open publishing platform. More and more B2B marketers started to follow Vajre's work, and a few more made a suggestion about creating an event around the concept.

Vajre states, "We put an event together in a couple of months and invited all top leaders in the marketplace that cared about the topic. Nothing to do with Terminus . . . not a single person spoke at the conference about Terminus. Ten sponsors [helped] to pay for the conference. . . . It was almost like . . . no real money spent [was] from us because it was all taken care of by the sponsorship(s). We were able to bring in 300 to 400 people to attend the conference. . . . and we were able to build relationships with all these top leaders. . . ."

The Flip My Funnel "Revenue Summit" became an instant success. After the first event, Terminus was able to close 15 significant customers directly from the event. Terminus then went on to launch events in cities around the country.

According to Vajre, the events themselves would have cost over $1.5 million to launch. The costs associated with the events were completely covered by outside sponsorships and registered attendees. Of the 300 total customers that Terminus currently has, 100 have come directly from the events.

Its 2017 conference was attended by more than 600 customers and prospects and was sponsored by large software companies such as Salesforce and Marketo (owned by Microsoft). Even direct competitors give Terminus money to sponsor the event because, as Vajre notes, Flip My Funnel is an industry event, not a Terminus event (similar to how Arrow positions its brands).

To make this work from an ongoing-process standpoint, Terminus has broken its marketing into two distinct parts, the Terminus Marketing Team and the Flip My Funnel Team, each with its own profit and loss (P&L) center.

Terminus sees more potential to grow and monetize the Flip My Funnel brand, and recently the company launched Flip My Funnel Account-Based Marketing University, in addition to an awards program.

Vajre believes that this model works because Terminus does not talk about itself. "I believe that one of the reasons we have been so successful is that we always talked about the problem. We never talked about ourselves at any given point . . . . we never ever talked about, 'here's what Terminus does and here's how Terminus can help you.' It was never that."

And if this model needs more validation, Vajre has actually been approached from outside investors to purchase the Flip My Funnel brand. That's correct—someone wants to buy Terminus's marketing division.

IT CANNOT JUST BE ABOUT CONTENT

In 1979, David Nussbaum graduated as a journalism major from Boston University and set out to become Robert Redford or Dustin Hoffman from the movie *All the President's Men*. David specifically loved print journalism and believed that was what he was going to do for the rest of his life—help tell amazing stories that people would read in the local or national newspaper.

But when David purchased his first computer in 1985, everything changed. He could immediately see how powerful this type of device could be for telling stories, and so he doubled down in this area, learning DOS, and then moved quickly into the Internet Age version 1.0.

Even though David was still dedicated to the idea of print journalism, he began to spend much more time understanding digital communications. It was at that same time that David started to see a business model emerging.

In the nineties, David became one of the leading experts around this new model, and in 2004 he became CEO of Penton Media, specifically brought in to turn around the ailing company. In 2000, Penton had been one of the shining stars of Wall Street—a fast-growing print media and events company whose stock was rising faster than the market.

Then, in 2001, after 9/11 and the dot-com bust, Penton went into a death spiral due to a series of poor acquisitions and then a massive debt burden. Within just two years, Penton's stock, which was $35 a share, dropped to 7 cents. David was brought in for sheer survival.

David was forced to look at Penton Media beyond the traditional business media model. Specifically, he organized the company, not around products, but around audiences. Penton's new goal was to focus not on what Penton had to sell to its readers, but instead on what readers wanted to (or would) buy.

I'll never forget a conversation I had with David in 2005. At that time, I reported directly to David, running Penton's Custom Media department. Our job was to sell custom content products to Penton advertisers that wanted to buy more than just advertising. In our first meeting David was crystal clear with his focus, saying, "Joe, I don't care if you sell shoes. Your job is to look at the assets you have to work with and monetize those assets."

David knew we had amazing relationships with our readers and customers. He also knew that Penton wouldn't survive by just selling more advertising. We had to change the model—and fast. And it worked. In 2007, Penton Media was sold to Prism Media at a valuation 10 times greater than what it was in 2004.

After succeeding at Penton, David moved on to F&W Media, a traditional publisher of special-interest media, such as arts and crafts, hunting, and antiques and collectibles. According to David: "Going back a bunch of years ago, my view was the content was the most important thing to be successful [in media]. But that's incorrect. As a media executive, you shouldn't pigeonhole yourself in delivering content in one way or another and focusing on just that but rather **focus on building a great community with phenomenal content.**"

At F&W, David helped move the focus from advertising to more of what the reader would buy. That meant evolving F&W into an e-commerce company. In seven years, F&W went from practically nothing to generating more than $60 million in direct, e-commerce revenues from its audiences, selling books, kits, memberships, subscriptions, and more.

And now today, David is CEO at America's Test Kitchen (ATK), where the entire company is funded without any support from advertisers. ATK monetizes its content and community through magazine subscriptions, website subscriptions, training courses, cookbooks, and recipe packs, as well as selling vast amounts of data and consultancy to larger organizations.

Currently, ATK is expanding its footprint by launching branded television shows in partnership with television networks, and then it will make money by selling brand-name products associated with each show.

David believes that ATK will be successful because it focuses on a particular niche like no one else does. "We're about the art and science of food and cooking. We don't compete with lifestyle brands," says David. "The Food Channel has growing competition among the lifestyle because they've moved away from being really about cooking to being about . . . competitions around cooking. It helps them get a larger audience but it doesn't help them get as dedicated and passionate an audience (as we have)."

Focusing on that core niche and content tilt is what helps ATK build a loyal audience, which then enables ATK to launch a number of products to monetize and activate that audience.

For David, his focus remains the same—build an amazingly loyal audience by delivering consistently valuable content experiences. From there, anything is possible.

THE MODEL, NOT A SUPPORT FUNCTION

Robert outlined "Content: The Business Model" perfectly in Chapter 1:

> It is the strategic use of content that will not only build audiences and drive the creation and retention of customers; it will do so at a profit. It will transform marketing as we know it today into something new. It will evolve the entire practice of marketing and can move some or all of the functions of marketing from cost center to profit center.

Most companies leverage content in their business to support other business goals, like demand generation or customer loyalty. And this is perfectly acceptable (at least for now). That is the essence of my book *Epic Content Marketing*.

But we cannot stop there. The marketers of tomorrow (at least the ones still around) will be running their entire marketing enterprise as its own business (like Victor Gao does at Arrow Electronics), not solely to support a business goal. Not only do the marketers of tomorrow need to understand marketing, but they need to understand publishing and how to run a media business like a CEO or publisher would.

The marketing department no longer needs to be limited to supporting certain products. Tomorrow's marketing department, once a loyal audience is built, will be able to create revenue and profit generation in almost limitless ways to add value to the organization.

But what does that business model look like from a revenue and profit standpoint? The next chapter will reveal all.

What's the use of running if you are not on the right road?

—German proverb

Profitable Insights

- The most innovative media companies and the enterprises that are leveraging content the best have exactly the same business model today (and yet not many see this).

- Whether you are a large company, like Red Bull or Arrow, or a small startup, like Terminus, the same model applies: build a loyal audience, and a number of direct revenue streams are possible.

- As David Nussbaum says, it's not about how much you publish; it's about building a loyal community. To do that, your content has to be phenomenal.

Profitable Resources

- Cosmopolitan Media Kit, accessed May 24, 2017, http://www.cosmomediakit.com/r5/home.asp.

- Exxon Mobil Guiding Principles, accessed May 24, 2017, http://corporate.exxonmobil.com/en/company/about-us/guiding-principles/our-guiding-principles.

- About Dennis Publishing, accessed May 24, 2017, http://www.dennis.co.uk/about/.

- "The Reinvention of Publishing: Media Firms Diversify to Survive," theguardian.com, accessed May 24, 2017, https://www.theguardian.com/media-network/2017/jan/30/reinvention-publishing-media-firms-diversify-survive.

- Brook Barnes, "Gwyneth Paltrow and Goop Go into the Fashion Business," nytimes.com, September 10, 2016, https://www.nytimes.com/2016/09/11/fashion/gwyneth-paltrow-goop-fashion-business.html?_r=0.

- Todd Zenger, "What Is the Theory of Your Firm?," *Harvard Business Review*, June 2013, https://hbr.org/2013/06/what-is-the-theory-of-your-firm.

- Red Bull Media House Media Kit, accessed May 24, 2017, https://www.redbullmediahouse.com/fileadmin/upload_media/content_licensing/Red_Bull_Media_House_Sales_Catalog_2015.pdf.

- Victor Gao, interview by Clare McDermott, January 2017.

- Mind of the Engineer Study, United Business Media, 2014.

- 2017 AspenCore Media Kit, accessed May 24, 2017, http://www.aspencore.com/AspenCoreMediaGuide.pdf.

- Sangram Vajre, interview by Clare McDermott, January 2017.

- David Nussbaum, interview by Clare McDermott, January 2017.

4

The Revenue Model

BY
JOE
PULIZZI

Randolph Duke: Money isn't everything, Mortimer.

Mortimer Duke: Oh, grow up.

Randolph Duke: Mother always said you were greedy.

Mortimer Duke: She meant it as a compliment.

—From the movie *Trading Places*, 1983

The investor of today does not profit from yesterday's growth.

—Warren Buffett

In May 2010 Content Marketing Institute (CMI) launched as an education and training organization for enterprise marketers, focusing on the approach of content marketing. That first full year, CMI generated a little less than $75,000 in total revenue (not profit, just revenue). In 2016, CMI revenues were in excess of $10 million at a healthy 25 percent net profit margin.

The model itself was pretty simple: CMI built a loyal audience of marketing professionals, from just a few thousand in 2010 to approximately 200,000 in 2016, and monetized those relationships in dozens of ways.

UNDER THE HOOD: CONTENT MARKETING INSTITUTE

CMI breaks down revenue into four different buckets: events, digital, print, and insights.

Events

When you look at CMI's business model, every digital, print, and research initiative leads, in one way or another, to our in-person training and events.

Content Marketing World

The largest and most profitable part of CMI's revenue model is in-person events. Content Marketing World, our flagship event, attracts over 4,000 delegates from 70 countries to Cleveland, Ohio, every September. The event offers 100 individual sessions for conference attendees, as well as a large exhibit hall featuring the latest in content marketing technologies.

The average attendee pays $1,295 to attend the main conference, while about 25 percent of attendees purchase what we call an "All Access" pass, where they also get two workshops and videos of all the presentations, which is about double the cost. The average sponsor invests approximately $15,000 for a booth or other sponsorship option, ranging from a few thousand dollars to $100,000. About 70 percent of the total event revenues come from attendee fees, and the other 30 percent are sponsorship fees.

Content Marketing World produces a gross margin in excess of 40 percent.

CMI also produces a smaller enterprise content event in Las Vegas called Intelligent Content Conference, which is attended by approximately 500 marketing professionals (CMI purchased Intelligent Content Conference in 2014). In addition, CMI produces "master class" events every fall in cities across the country. In 2017, CMI toured eight cities, where the events were attended by between 50 and 100 individuals at each location.

Digital

When CMI was first launching its business model, it was the digital revenue streams that led the way.

Benefactors

In 2010, the "benefactor" sponsorship was the first CMI revenue generator. It's a combination of advertising, sponsorship, and content for companies that want to reach CMI's target audience via the website, which now attracts over one million visitors every year. The first year, CMI charged $15,000 for an annual sponsorship. In 2017, that number was $40,000, limited to 10 companies during a 12-month period.

A benefactor sponsorship includes the following:

- Ability to create educational blog posts to distribute on CMI's website (that must be approved by CMI editorial staff)

- 12 months of online banner display advertising (10 percent of CMI visitors will see the benefactor's advertising unit on an ongoing basis)

- Ad inclusion in weekly CMI e-newsletters and daily blog alerts (minimum 40 per year)

- Branding on footer of every CMI website page

- First chance at special partnerships and opportunities

Podcast

In November 2013, Robert and I talked shop on the phone for about an hour. At the end of the conversation, Robert said, "That was a great chat . . . we should have recorded that." The next week, we launched the CMI podcast *This Old Marketing*, where we critiqued the news of the week. We mirrored the show's format from ESPN's *Pardon the Interruption* program.

That first month, the podcast generated 1,000 downloads. Robert and I were amazed that 1,000 people actually took the time to listen to the hour-long program. By the beginning of 2017, the podcast generated approximately 100,000 downloads per month. Every week, an episode is published Monday night (eastern time), and show notes are published as a blog post on the CMI site every Saturday (Figure 4.1). For each episode, there is one main sponsor, which submits an educational piece of content for Robert and me to discuss and promote. Monthly revenue ranges from $6,000 to $10,000 (at times, CMI has two sponsors an episode).

Email List Rental

Many of CMI's opt-in e-newsletter subscribers also sign up to receive relevant partner messages. Every Thursday, a CMI partner purchases the CMI email list to promote a white paper, e-book, or some other valuable piece of information for marketers. CMI delivers this on the partner's behalf and charges around $300 CPM (cost per thousand).

Figure 4.1	*This Old Marketing* podcast downloads have steadily increased since 2013.

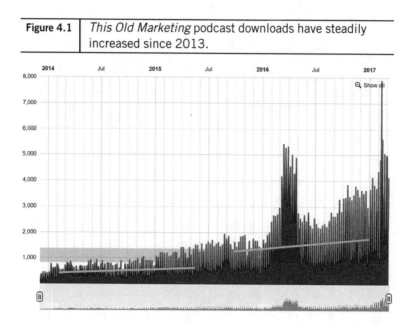

Webinars

Every month, CMI produces three sponsored educational webinars for the CMI audience. Each webinar attracts between 500 and 1,000 registrations, of which approximately 40 percent attend the live event. CMI works with each sponsor to make sure the content of the webinar is aligned with the attendees' needs, as well as the goals of the sponsor. The average webinar is an investment of $19,000.

White Papers

CMI houses a white paper library to promote its partners' helpful educational content. These white papers are generally between 8 and 12 pages, and readers can download them free in exchange for the reader's email address. That means that the readers are giving the sponsor permission to contact them (via email) in exchange for the valuable information provided in the white paper.

Virtual Event

Every February, CMI produces a live, free virtual event called ContentTECH, where the spotlight is on the latest in content marketing technology. In 2017, CMI saw 4,000 registered attendees and 12 sponsors supporting the event, bringing in over $100,000 in total revenue to CMI.

Print

Chief Content Officer Magazine

Chief Content Officer (*CCO*) magazine was launched in January 2011. As of 2017, *CCO* has delivered 30 issues to 20,000 marketers for each issue, with about 60 percent of the audience receiving a print version and the remainder receiving a digital version. *CCO* is critical to CMI's overall strategy since the content of the magazine and the content of the original platform (the blog) are fully integrated.

The original idea for *CCO* was to reach chief marketing officers and other senior marketers that had budgetary responsibility for content marketing. The strategy was simple. Get the magazine into their hands, and they would begin to see content marketing as a valuable go-to-market strategy and start funding content resources within the enterprise.

CMI's general folio (page count) is between 40 and 64 pages. The cost depends on the number of total pages, number of editorial pages, and total print count, but generally CMI's hard costs of producing the publication are a minimum $40,000 per issue. CMI's partners purchase full-page and half-page advertisements in every issue, and a handful of international marketers pay to receive the magazine abroad. Generally, each issue generates a small profit for CMI.

Understanding a Print Budget

Understanding the budgeting behind what makes a magazine work is critical. Areas to consider include:

- **Project management.** The fee for someone to oversee the production of the magazine.
- **Editorial.** Raw content costs (including outside contributors), managing editorial costs, and proofreading fees.
- **Design.** Someone to lay out the graphics for the publication.
- **Photos and illustrations.** Investment in any photo shoots or custom graphic creation.
- **Database fees.** Charges to make sure your audience list is postal ready.
- **Printing.** Cost to print the publication.
- **Postage.** Post office fees to deliver each issue.
- **Shipping.** Any bulk shipping fees from the printer to your office location.
- **Commissions.** If your magazine is supported though advertising revenue, you'll need to pay a commission to the salesperson. Commission rates are generally 8 to 10 percent for one of your staff and up to 20 to 25 percent to hire a freelance salesperson who covers all his or her own costs.

Insights

CMI's Insights group is our ancillary revenue, which includes online training, advisory services, research, and awards.

Online Training

CMI launched an online training program in 2015 specifically to deliver education and training to those marketing professionals that could not attend one of CMI's in-person events like Content Marketing World. CMI University is open for enrollment four times per year (as quarterly semesters) and requires an annual investment of $995 per person. In addition, CMI sells corporate packages to companies that want to educate their entire marketing department. To date, over 1,000 marketing professionals have registered and completed the coursework.

Advisory Services

Although CMI delivers educational content on the approach of content marketing every day, some companies require a "hands-on" approach. CMI has worked with companies such as AT&T, Petco, the Gates Foundation, Capital Group, Citrix, SAS, Dell, Adobe, Abbott, and more on customized training sessions. These in-person advisory sessions are priced between $15,000 and $45,000 per engagement, depending on the deliverables.

Research

More websites link to CMI's original research than anything else CMI has ever produced. In 2009 CMI partnered with MarketingProfs to create and distribute an annual benchmark study around the approach of content marketing. The research is fielded in June every year. CMI releases the initial results during Content Marketing World (September) each year and then publishes sub-reports for the next 12 months, including B2B, B2C, nonprofit, enterprise, small business, manufacturing, and more.

Each report becomes a 40-page e-book and is sponsored by a CMI partner (at approximately $15,000 per report). In addition, CMI produces small research projects for leading brands, where CMI fields the study to its audience and then creates and distributes the report. These sponsored reports range from $20,000 to $40,000 per project.

Content Marketing Awards

In 2012, Content Marketing Institute partnered with an outside agency that owned a content marketing awards program called the Magnum Opus Awards. These awards were the largest awards program in the industry, and CMI was compensated on an affiliate revenue basis for promoting the awards program (CMI received a percentage of revenue on every submission).

In 2014, CMI purchased the Magnum Opus Awards program outright and renamed it the Content Marketing Awards. Each year, over 400 organizations submit more than 1,200 entries, and CMI works with 100 volunteer judges in 91 content marketing categories. The awards program generates approximately $400,000 in total revenue, as well as countless content creation opportunities and amazing insight into the industry.

• • •

To sum up, Content Marketing Institute has been able to monetize its loyal audience in over a dozen ways at a high growth rate, while at the same time, each initiative works to help market other profitable CMI offerings (the webinars promote the in-person events, the in-person events promote the awards, etc.). CMI believes that once a loyal audience/community can be created and nurtured, nearly any relevant product or service could, in theory, be launched as a profitable venture, as long as CMI continues to deliver on its promise to readers.

THE MEDIA MARKETING REVENUE MODEL

As discussed in Chapter 3, the new marketing model and the new media model are one and the same. Once a loyal audience is devel-

| **Figure 4.2** | The media marketing revenue model: 10 ways that an organization can drive revenues from a loyal audience. |

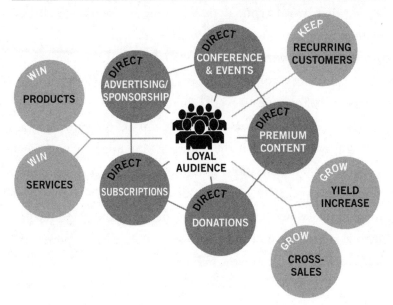

oped, there are 10 distinct ways to monetize that audience (five directly and five indirectly satisfying Win, Keep, or Grow goals), as shown in Figure 4.2.

DIRECT REVENUE

There are five different methods by which companies can directly generate revenues from an audience group: advertising/sponsorship, conferences and events, premium content offerings, donations, and subscriptions.

Advertising/Sponsorship

The most popular method of driving direct revenues is through advertising and sponsorship programs: companies willing to pay you for direct access to your audience.

Traditional Advertising

- **Ann Reardon.** The YouTube baking queen, who now has over three million subscribers to her YouTube channel "How to Cook That," makes the majority of her revenues from collecting YouTube advertising royalties. With very few resources, Ann was able to differentiate her message by focusing on what she calls "impossible food creations."

- **The Society of Fire Protection Engineers (SFPE).** SFPE, the leading association for fire protection engineers, delivers its print magazine, *Fire Protection Engineering*, to 13,000 members and subscribers each quarter, generating a healthy profit through traditional print magazine advertising. The association uses the funds from the profit to invest in research and educational programming.

- **Red Box.** The popular DVD delivery service that sits within or outside physical retail stores offers an e-newsletter to customers focused on new movie and game releases. Each newsletter includes one or multiple sponsors (generally promoting their own games and movies) that pay Red Box to reach its audience.

- **Kraft Foods.** Kraft Foods (owned by Kraft Heinz) owns one of the leading collections of food brands in the world, KraftRecipes.com. Kraft employs 20 culinary professionals who work with Kraft products every day. There are well over 30,000 recipes on the company's website, where Kraft generates direct revenue from advertising on the site, as well as print advertising in its magazine, *Kraft Food & Family*.

Native Advertising/Sponsored Content

Sharethrough defines native advertising as a form of paid media where the ad experience follows the natural form and function of the user experience in which it is placed. In simple terms, the advertisement looks like the content. This could be paid content that looks like an article on a media site, or it might be a post on LinkedIn that looks exactly like all the other updates from the people you follow.

Even the largest media brands in the world, like the *Wall Street Journal*, are generating substantial revenues from sponsored content. According to the *New York Times*, young media companies such as Vice generate the majority of their revenues from sponsored content, while the *Atlantic* and *Slate* both say that sponsored content is over 50 percent of their digital revenue stream.

Native advertising/sponsored content is growing as a part of the larger advertising sector for a few reasons:

- Media brands and social platforms (like LinkedIn and Facebook) are aggressively offering native advertising products.

- Brands now spend approximately 25 to 30 percent of their budget on content marketing initiatives. Brands have started to make this a priority, so native advertising is seen as a viable opportunity.

- When done right, it can work. For example, the majority of BuzzFeed's revenues are through native advertising, and this strategy has been so successful that the company has been able to generate revenues at a substantial premium over traditional online advertising.

- There is a renewed passion in the advertising community around native. This "new advertising" (even though it's not really new at all) has given hope to media buyers around the world that something can perform better than a banner ad.

Some examples of sponsored content in action include:

- **Forbes.** Large companies, such as SAP, pay *Forbes* a monthly fee for the opportunity to publish content that looks like editorial content as part of the *Forbes* BrandVoice program. These programs run upward of $75,000 per month for sponsors.

- **Conan O'Brien.** Conan and his Team Coco have been producing sponsored content placements on his late night show for years now. In one situation, Conan and sidekick Andy Richter talk about their "Cyber Monday" issues, which result in a pitch for PayPal.

- **The Onion.** The satirical website drives most of its revenues from content programs like "Woman Going to Take Quick Break After Filling Out Name, Address on Tax Forms," which was underwritten by H&R Block (see Figure 4.3).

Sponsorships

While an advertisement generally involves interrupting a user's experience with a product or content promotion, a sponsorship underwrites a piece of content, generally by one company. The benefits of sponsorships include leads (a sponsored download) and/or brand awareness (sponsoring a podcast or television program).

Figure 4.3	The satirical news network The Onion offers sponsored content opportunities to a number of its partners—in this case, H&R Block.

- **Content Marketing Institute** (CMI). CMI favors a sponsorship model over an advertising model for the majority of its products.
  - Podcast—each episode has an individual sponsor.
  - Research reports—each report has one sponsor.
  - Webinars—each webinar is sponsored by a single sponsor.

- **ESPN's** *Mike & Mike.* The popular morning radio and television show (syndicated on radio and televised live on

ESPN2) has been sponsored by Progressive Insurance for years. ESPN does this with a number of its live shows, including *Pardon the Interruption (PTI)*, which is generally sponsored by Captain Morgan or another alcoholic beverage company.

Conferences and Events

According to CMI/MarketingProfs research, approximately 7 in 10 enterprises create and manage their own events. Some of these are small client gatherings, while others are full-scale events with exhibition halls and concurrent sessions. Revenues are driven, for the most part, through paid registration to the event or sponsorships, such as parties or exhibition space.

- **The Chicken Whisperer.** Andy Schneider is the backyard poultry king and has become the go-to resource for anything and everything chickens. As Andy began to raise chickens in his Atlanta-area backyard, he began to sell them to his friends directly and then on Craigslist. There were many who were interested in raising their own chickens, but they needed a lot of education just to get started. So Andy formed a "meetup" in Atlanta to answer questions from those interested in backyard poultry.

  From there, Andy grew the Chicken Whisperer platform into a book, a magazine (with over 60,000 subscribers), and a radio show, which has now run for over seven years with more than 20,000 weekly subscribers. He also travels around the country doing road shows, the main part of his revenue mix, which are exclusively sponsored by Kalmbach Feeds, his major financial supporter.

- **Minecon.** Minecon is the official event of Minecraft, the online multiplayer building game owned by Microsoft. In 2016, the annual event attracted a sold-out 12,000 attendees (at $160 per ticket, tickets sold out in minutes) as well as an exhibition hall featuring the latest Minecraft technology and merchandising (where Microsoft accepts booth fees from sponsors and partners).

- **Lennox Live.** Lennox is one of the largest manufacturers of heating and air conditioning equipment in the world. Every year, it attracts the leading contractors and distributors from around the United States, offering education around technology, marketing, and business practices. Exhibiting partners include companies such as Honeywell, Cintas, and Fluke. Lennox generates revenue directly from attendee fees, as well as more than a dozen manufacturing and service partners.

- **Adobe Summit.** Adobe Summit holds one of the largest digital marketing events on the planet. In 2017, Adobe attracted more than 10,000 attendees to learn about the latest in digital marketing technology. Sponsors included Accenture, Deloitte, Microsoft, and IBM. Full price for attendee registration was $1,895 per person. This one event easily generates more than $10 million in revenue for Adobe.

Premium Content

Premium content packages come in a number of forms, including direct-for-sale content products, funded content purchased on demand, and syndicated content opportunities.

Content Products

- **Digital Photography School (DPS).** Darren Rowse launched DPS as the leading source for beginning photographers and how they can get the most out of their picture-taking skills. DPS generates millions per year by developing premium e-books and specialty reports for direct sale. DPS's premium content sales have become core to the company's monetization strategy.

- **BuzzFeed (*Tasty*).** BuzzFeed's time-lapsed cooking videos have been viewed by over 40 billion (billion with a *b*) times in the past two years. One of the ways BuzzFeed monetizes that success is through customized cookbooks. In 2016, BuzzFeed launched *Tasty: The Cookbook*, a hardcopy book that can be customized by buyers depending on their recipe tastes. In just a few weeks, BuzzFeed sold over 100,000 copies of the cookbook.

Funded Content Sales

- **Cleveland Clinic.** The Cleveland Clinic, one of the largest hospital networks in the world, has become one of the leading healthcare publishers in the world through its platform *The Health Hub*. Because of that expertise, Google has approached the Cleveland Clinic to create written content on specific healthcare topics that Google felt provided inadequate search results.

- **Foodable TV.** This organization publishes a number of documentaries and food series, which are developed and then purchased by companies like Netflix and Amazon Prime.

Syndicated Content

Content syndication happens when originally created content is published to third-party websites for a fee.

- **Red Bull.** Red Bull's "Content Pool" contains thousands of videos, photography, and music that media companies and content producers can purchase rights to directly from Red Bull.

- **Yahoo! News.** Although Yahoo! has a full editorial department to create original content, much of what you'll find on Yahoo!'s site is syndicated content paid directly to companies like MSNBC, Newsweek, and Reuters.

Donations

Generally, donations work best when they subsidize the publishing of not-for-profit and cause organizations.

- ***America's Test Kitchens.*** *America's Test Kitchens* and *Cook's Country* are television programs on public broadcasting, and both shows have sponsor underwriters that *almost* cover the entire cost of production.

- ***Penn Stater*** **magazine (Penn State University).** The *Penn Stater*, Penn State University Alumni Association's magazine, has been published since 1910 and is delivered every other month to Penn State alumni (including myself). The reason the magazine exists is to drive direct donations to support the Alumni Association and the university itself.

- **Pro Publica.** Pro Publica (http://www.propublica.org/) is a nonprofit organization that uses its funding to develop investigative journalism that it deems is important for the public to hear. Founded by Paul Steiger, former managing editor of the *Wall Street Journal*, Pro Publica employs over 50 journalists and receives its major funding from the Sandler Corporation, which committed funding for multiple years upon Pro Publica's launch in June 2008. Pro Publica also accepts ongoing donations from anyone that believes in the organization's cause.

- ■ **Charity Water.** Charity Water's inspirational storytelling has enabled the organization to raise more than $150 million in the last five years.

Micro-Funding

Kevin Kelly wrote an amazing (and now very popular) essay in 2008 called "1,000 True Fans." In it, he describes a number of examples of how writers funded their way to publishing. Today, this is much easier to do through programs like Kickstarter and GoFundMe. In the essay, Kelly distills this example from Lawrence Evans:

> In 2004 author Lawrence Watt-Evans used [micro-funding] to publish his newest novel. He asked his True Fans to collectively pay $100 per month. When he got $100 he posted the next chapter of the novel. The entire book was published online for his True Fans, and then later in paper for all his fans. He is now writing a second novel this way.

Subscriptions

Subscriptions differ from premium content in that subscriptions, paid for by the consumer, promise to deliver content ongoing, over a period of time (generally a year).

- ***New York Times.*** A major part of the turnaround at the *New York Times* (from diminishing print advertising) is its growth in digital subscribers to the newspaper. According to Quartz, the *New York Times* has added approximately one million digital subscribers over the past two years, with 276,000 in growth (its biggest growth since launching the subscriber program) after the election of President Donald Trump.

- **Schneider Electric's Energy University.** As Robert already discussed, Schneider Electric launched Energy University 10 years ago as a free online educational resource that provides an extensive library of training videos about energy usage, technical developments in various industries, management solutions to energy consumption challenges, and other energy-related topics. It contains almost 500 courses and has over 500,000 subscribers, who have taken over 750,000 courses since the website was launched. The courses are translated into different languages, giving Energy University a global reach. Its impact includes acting as a source of new business for the company, providing insights into customer needs in regional markets, helping Schneider recruit new employees, and, of course, educating people about developments in the field of electrical engineering. Recently, Schneider has started to sell components of Energy University as a subscription. Early reports are positive.

INDIRECT REVENUE

While direct revenue options have been traditionally thought of as part of the media company model, indirect revenues fall under the approach known as content marketing, or creating content and building relationships with audiences to fund organizational business goals.

WIN REVENUE

Win revenue includes the creation and distribution of content with the goal of selling specific products or services.

Products

Examples of organizations selling products to their loyal audiences include:

- **Chili Klaus.** Claus Pilgaard, aka Chili Klaus, is one of the most well-known celebrity figures in Denmark, all because of the extraordinary way he talks about chili peppers. Claus's YouTube videos have garnered millions of views, including one where Claus conducts the Danish National Chamber Orchestra playing "Tango Jalousie" while eating the world's hottest chili peppers. That video alone has seen more than three million views (note that this is more than half the population of Denmark).

  From this success, Claus has launched a suite of successful products under the brand "Chili Klaus" including chili chips, chili sauce, chili licorice, and dozens of other products.

- **Indium Corporation.** Indium, a global manufacturing company headquartered in upstate New York, develops and manufactures materials used primarily in the electronics assembly industry. At its core, the company develops soldering materials to keep electronic components from coming apart.

Rick Short, Indium's director of marketing communications, knew that Indium employees had more knowledge about industrial soldering equipment than just about any other company in the world. This makes sense: soldering is the knowledge area where Indium manufactures most of its products. Indium believed that if it published its expertise on a regular basis, it would draw in new customers and have opportunities to sell more products. Today Indium, through its blog *From One Engineer to Another*, has over 70 blogs and 21 bloggers. Simply put, this blog is how it goes to market today and is central to the company's ongoing growth.

- **Copyblogger.** Brian Clark launched Copyblogger in 2006 as an educational resource for online copyrighting. Over the next few years, Copyblogger generated over 100,000 subscribers to its daily blog content. A few years later, Copyblogger launched the content management system Rainmaker. Over 90 percent of the sales of Rainmaker come from Copyblogger subscribers. Today, Rainmaker is one of the fastest-growing marketing software-as-a-service products on the market.

- **L'Oreal (Makeup.com).** L'Oreal, the global makeup conglomerate, purchased Makeup.com from Live Current Media for over $1 million back in 2010. According to McKinsey, L'Oreal has leveraged the idea of teaching consumers how to apply makeup correctly, and the result has been starting relationships with possible customers at much earlier times in the buyers' journey.

- **Sony's Alpha Universe.** Sony's Alpha Universe is a content platform dedicated to photography professionals, but it doesn't focus on Sony products; it focuses on educational and helpful information. After starting with a blog, Sony has diversified into a podcast and training university. The site's purpose is to drive product sales for Sony's Alpha line of cameras.

- **Moz.** Rand Fishkin, CEO of Moz (originally called SEOMoz), started his blog on search engine optimization insights back in 2004. In less than five years, Moz had over 100,000 email subscribers.

  Rand originally monetized the audience through consulting services, but in 2007, Moz launched a beta subscription service for software tools and reports. By 2009, Moz closed the consulting business entirely and focused on selling software to its audience, turning Moz into a $30 million organization by 2015.

- **Missouri Star Quilt Company.** Jenny Doan is the cofounder of the Missouri Star Quilt Co., a quilt shop in Hamilton that boasts the largest selection of precut fabrics in the world. To spur sagging sales, Jenny created quilting video tutorials to post on YouTube.

  The channel received 1,000 subscribers in its first year, 10,000 in year two, and today has over 350,000 subscribers. Jenny's videos have reached as many as a two million views. The videos have driven new traffic to her website, gaining an average of 2,000 online sales per day and making the company the world's largest supplier of precut fabrics.

Products—Affiliate Sales

- **Entrepreneur on Fire (EOF).** EOF is a popular daily podcast series run by John Lee Dumas. John promotes a number of companies that pay an affiliate fee to John on either click or actual sale of product. EOF publishes its revenues and profits every month on its blog. Here is a sample of just its affiliate income for the month of February 2017.

Affiliate Income: $91,155

Resources for Entrepreneurs: $73,098

- Audible: $172
- AWeber: $104
- Bluehost: $600 *(step-by-step guide and 23 WordPress tutorials)*
- ClickFunnels: $64,892
- Coaching Referrals: $4,775
- Disclaimer Template: $44 *(legal disclaimers for your website)*
- Easy Webinar: $438
- Fizzle: $837
- Leadpages: $1,088
- SamCart: $148

Courses for Entrepreneurs: $15,371

- DSG's Create Awesome Online Courses: $8,245
- Eben Pagan's Launch Blueprint: $635
- Michael Hyatt's Your Best Year Ever: $4,234
- Nick Stephenson's Your First 10k Readers: $306
- Tribe: Create Recurring Revenue: $1,432
- Bryan Harris' 10k Subscribers: $519

Resources for Podcasters: $915

- Libsyn: $730
- Pat Flynn's Smart Podcast Player: $120
- UDemy Podcasting Course: $65

Other Resources: $1,771

- Amazon Associates: $1,227
- Other: $544

■ **The Wirecutter.** The Wirecutter, the gadget and deal listing site, was purchased by the *New York Times* in 2016 for $30 million. The site makes a little bit of money every time a product recommended on the site is sold. And these deals add up—in 2015, the company generated over $150 million from affiliate revenues.

Products—Data

If there is a product that is easiest for media companies to sell, it's data. With access to audiences, and the behavior of those audiences, an organization can package and sell that information in multiple ways.

■ **GIE Media.** GIE is a trade media company with audiences in the lawn and landscape industry (among others). Each year, it invests heavily in its subscription database and knows pretty much all the buyers and influencers around key product areas. GIE then sells access to that data to large brands on a one-time and subscription model.

■ **Advance Publications.** Advance is one of the largest privately held media companies in the United States, holding hundreds of entities including Reddit, Pitchfork, and Charter Communications. The result of this gives the company insight into over 50 million people. From that, Advance can sell organizations in multiple industries data on specific audiences, including market share, path to purchase data, and how and what a customer base buys, as well as local data information and trends for retailers.

Services

- *Game Theory.* Matthew Patrick created the idea of *Game Theory* while watching an online program on learning through gaming. *Game Theory* became a weekly YouTube video series that combined Matthew's passion for gaming and video games with his skill set of math and analytics.

  After 56 episodes over a one-year time frame, Matthew had an audience of 500,000 YouTube subscribers interested in his take on how math works in gaming. For example, his episode "How PewDiePie [an online video celebrity] Conquered YouTube" generated more than five million views. His episode "Why the Official Zelda Timeline Is Wrong" saw more than four million downloads.

  Today, Matthew Patrick's Game Theory brand has well over eight million subscribers. From this success, Matthew launched Theorists Inc., a specialty consulting firm that works with large brands that want to be successful on YouTube. Theorists Inc. has been hired directly by some of the biggest YouTube stars on the planet to help them attract more viewers, as well as has been hired by a number of Fortune 500 companies. Even the mighty YouTube itself hired Theorists to consult directly to help YouTube retain and grow its audience numbers.

- **Zappos Insights.** Zappos, the shoe company purchased by Amazon.com, launched Zappos Insights as a separate business entity under the Zappos brand. As CEO Tony Hsieh's story of cultural transformation (through his book and speaking) became more popular, Zappos started to get more requests for help in the cultural transformation area. As more and more companies contacted Zappos, its leaders simply could not keep up with the demand, and saw the business opportunity in front of them. Zappos Insights offers consulting, training, advisory, and mentoring services as part of its product suite.

KEEP REVENUE

Of all the revenue drivers of this approach, Keep revenue, or loyalty, is the oldest of them all and is still extremely important today. Organizations of all sizes originally launched print magazines to keep the loyalty of their customers over time.

- **John Deere's *The Furrow* magazine.** John Deere launched *The Furrow* magazine in 1895. It is still published today, produced in print and digital format in 14 different languages and distributed to 40 countries. *The Furrow* has always focused on how farmers can learn the latest technology to grow their farms and businesses. Over the past 100 years, just a handful of the articles have been about John Deere products and services.

- *LEGO Club Magazine.* In the 1980s and 1990s, LEGO faced a tremendous threat from competing construction toys, and the company knew it needed to build a powerhouse brand and integrated marketing approach to go up against these building-block imitators. Among its incredible branding and content marketing initiatives is the *LEGO Club Magazine*, which is customized for subscribers by local market and age. The magazine allows kids of any age to receive targeted content that's relevant to them in a fun, portable format. As an extension of its LEGO Club offering (one of the biggest and most popular children's member clubs in the world), LEGO worked hard to improve its magazine product in 2011 with more cartoon stories of the LEGO bricks in action, better integration of customer photos, and some awesome in-store programs at LEGO store outlets and its new Master Builder Academy.

LEGO Club Magazine was originally launched as *Brick Kicks* in 1987 (I was a subscriber).

GROW REVENUE

Once a customer is acquired, innovative companies leverage that customer's data to deliver targeted and consistent publications to, in essence, create better customers over time.

Yield Increase

- *thinkMoney* **from TD Ameritrade.** While you may think investing services equals conservative and buttoned-down (especially in complex derivatives markets), *thinkMoney* follows a different approach. It takes the subject of investing seriously, but it doesn't take itself with the grim seriousness of many Wall Street firms. Instead, *thinkMoney* embraces a "sophisticated simplicity" approach that's edgy without being flippant, and witty without being irreverent.

  thinkMoney reaches more than 200,000 active trade customers, and according to surveys, the average customer engages with the magazine for 45 minutes or more per sitting. More than 80 percent of readers take some meaningful action after reading, and those subscribers who engage in the publication trade five times more than those who do not.

Cross-Sales

- **Fold Factory.** Trish Witkowski, CEO of Fold Factory, has become a celebrity in the direct mailing industry through her regular video show, *The 60-Second Super Cool Fold of the Week*, where she details amazing examples of print direct mail. According to author and speaker Andrew Davis, "Her 250-plus videos have yielded over a million views and more than 5,000 subscribers. In addition, Trish has become a spokesperson for a number of brands, tours the world as a speaker, and conducts workshops."

  The Fold Factory videos have been directly responsible for over $500,000 in additional revenue.

• • •

The most successful organizations in the future will leverage not one part, but multiple parts of the media marketing model. Just as investors diversify their portfolios with multiple stocks and/ or mutual funds, so do companies need to diversify the revenue streams generated from their marketing.

Profitable Insights

- Once a loyal community is built and an organization has direct access to an audience, there are 10 discrete ways to generate revenue from that audience.

- In general, organizations start by leveraging one specific revenue source from a particular audience, and then, once that matures, the organizations begin to diversify their revenue streams into other areas.

- Traditionally, media companies leverage direct revenue sources, while brands that sell products and services generate indirect sources of revenue. In the future, the majority of both media and non-media companies will use the same model and generate both types of revenue.

Profitable Resources

- Andrew Jack, "There Are at Least Eight Promising Business Models for Email Newsletters," neimanlab.org, November 10, 2016, http://www.niemanlab.org/2016/11/there-are-at-least-eight-promising-business-models-for-email-newsletters/.

- Redbox Email Subscription Form, accessed on May 24, 2017, https://www.redbox.com/email.

- John Herrman, "How Sponsored Content Is Becoming King in a Facebook World," nytimes.com, July 24, 2016, https://www.nytimes.com/2016/07/25/business/sponsored-content-takes-larger-role-in-media-companies.html?_r=0.

- "Conan's Sweater Gets Stolen," teamcoco.com, December 4, 2014, 2017, http://teamcoco.com/video/conan-stolen-sweater/.

- Dan Shewan, "Native Advertising Examples: 5 of the Best (and Worst)," wordstream.com, last updated March 10, 2017, http://www.wordstream.com/blog/ws/2014/07/07/native-advertising-examples.

- Claus Pilgaard, interview by Clare McDermott, January 2015.

- Andy Schneider, interview by Clare McDermott, January 2015.

- Nate Birt, "The Do's and Don'ts of Content Syndication," scribblelive.com, May 31, 2016, http://www.scribblelive.com/blog/2016/05/31/dos-donts-content-syndication/.

- "1,000 True Fans," kk.org, accessed on May 24, 2017, http://kk.org/thetechnium/1000-true-fans/.

- Ashley Rodriguez and Zameena Mejia, "Thanks to Trump, the *New York Times* Added More Subscribers in Three Months Than in All of 2015," qz.com, February 3, 2017, https://qz.com/901684/thanks-to-trump-the-new-york-times-added-more-subscribers-in-three-months-than-in-all-of-2015/.

- "EOFire's February 2017 Income Report," eofire.com, accessed May 24, 2017, https://www.eofire.com/income42/.

- David Court, Dave Elzinga, Bo Finneman, and Jesko Perrey, "The New Battleground for Marketing-Led Growth," *McKinsey Quarterly*, February 2017,

Profitable Resources *(continued)*

http://www.mckinsey.com/business-functions/marketing
-and-sales/our-insights/the-new-battleground-for
-marketing-led-growth.

- Laura Hazard Owen, "Think the Wirecutter Invented
  Affiliate Revenue? Meet the Mom Who's Been Doing It
  Since 2010," NiemanLab, February 17, 2017, http://
  www.niemanlab.org/2017/02/think-the-wirecutter
  -invented-affiliate-revenue-meet-the-mom-whos-been
  -doing-it-since-2010/.

- Crista Foley (Zappos), interview by Clare McDermott,
  January 2017.

5

The Marketing Media Savings Model

BY
ROBERT
ROSE

An investment in knowledge pays the best interest.

—Benjamin Franklin

My problem lies in reconciling my gross habits with my net income.

—Errol Flynn

One of the most common TV tropes is the "enhance video" scene. You've seen it a million times: the detective and the technology specialist watch grainy security camera surveillance footage, and the detective notices something strange. "Enhance that bit," he says. The technology specialist zooms in on the license plate. There's something there. "Clear it up and enhance it more," says the detective. And then, magically, that black smudge reflected in the water droplet on the license plate of the car becomes a recognizable face. They've discovered the killer's identity, captured with a security camera that barely records at a resolution of Super 8 film. It's become so ridiculous that in one episode of the FOX show

Bones, one of the technicians scans a skeleton, into whose bones the villains had carved a hand-coded "fractal virus." Somehow, the scanner is magically programmed to both read and automatically execute any code it finds in bones, and the virus is automatically uploaded into the computer, causing (and I'm serious here) the computer to catch fire. Yup. Ridiculous.

But here's a fun fact. These capabilities are becoming real. In 2014, scientists staged a passport photo setting with a high-definition camera. They placed a few people in front of the subject, and when they zoomed in, they could make out all the people standing behind the camera. They enhanced the photo and zoomed in, and you could make out, quite distinctly, each individual face. All the fun we've had at the expense of these cop shows may be about to come full circle. The technology is getting good enough to do exactly what we've been laughing about.

It's an interesting metaphor for where we are as we look to completely redefine our marketing functions today. In many cases these days, the capabilities of technology have completely outpaced our imagination and ability to make use of the technology. Marketing can, and frequently does, purchase technology that we simply don't understand at all. So, our marketing efforts these days can become completely focused on being more efficient at understanding all the features that can be had with the use of software, rather than how we are solving the real challenges of our customers.

And as software becomes more sophisticated, our focus on chasing the technology tail is only becoming more pronounced. One recent study found that only 8 percent of marketers believe that they have all the tools they need and that they utilize them to their fullest extent. Thirty-three percent of marketers believe that they don't have all the tools they need but that they fully utilize the ones they have. The next largest group—34 percent—of these marketers believe that they don't have all the tools they need *and* that they don't fully utilize the ones they already have.

This matches up well with research that we conducted in 2016 at Content Marketing Institute. We looked specifically at content-related technologies and found that only 18 percent of marketers felt like they had the right technologies to manage their owned media properties in the business. Another 45 percent said that they had tools, but weren't using them to their potential. Then, further, when we asked these marketers what their number one priority was for educational needs regarding content—it was overwhelmingly (66 percent) to learn how to better use technology.

Marketers are under increasing pressure to get more and more effectiveness out of our communication efforts—and technology is only adding to the investment burden of the cost. We must find better and more strategic ways to get more effectiveness (as opposed to efficiency) out of what we're doing with data and technology.

THE NEW MARKETING MEDIA SAVINGS MODEL

As Joe outlined in the previous chapter, there are many opportunities to start driving growth and revenue with owned media. But there are also a good number of efficiencies that can be driven as well. When we look more closely at technology and the value of data to our marketing efforts, we can begin to see that audiences can provide a means of many of the other things we need to accomplish as a business in a more effective and efficient manner. Combined with the revenue and growth to the bottom line, these cost savings can help us to achieve a much more profitable business.

Consider Kraft Foods for a moment. It has been a leader in content marketing for a number of years. It publishes *Food & Family Magazine*—a revenue-generating magazine that consistently beats *Food & Wine* in terms of circulation. But the real magic isn't the revenue the content drives; it's the cost savings for Kraft's traditional digital media buy. The company utilizes the data that it pulls from the audience of its Online Recipes database and achieves a four-times return on its traditional digital media buy.

Using its content and data technology, Kraft tracks more than 22,000 attributes of the more than 100 million visitors to its website. That's two trillion data points if you're counting at home. Utilizing that data, the company personalizes traditional digital advertisements and focuses the advertisements through much more programmatic media buys. As Julie Fleischer, the then director for data, content, and media, told *Ad Age* in 2014:

> The days of free organic reach are rapidly coming to an end. If you wouldn't spend money behind it, then why do it? It's shouting into the wind without making a sound. . . . Relevant content programmed strategically with your advertising makes your advertising work harder for you.

As discussed in Chapter 3, the new marketing model and the new media model are one and the same (Figure 5.1). Once a loyal audience is developed, we can look to seven ways to monetize that audience to help save costs. Like the revenue models, these also map to the Grow, Keep, and Win framework.

Decrease Sales Costs

One of the biggest opportunities from looking at the value of a loyal audience is in how it can decrease the cost of sale.

One B2B technology company that we worked with had built an efficient direct marketing lead generation engine by leveraging,

Figure 5.1	Marketing media savings model

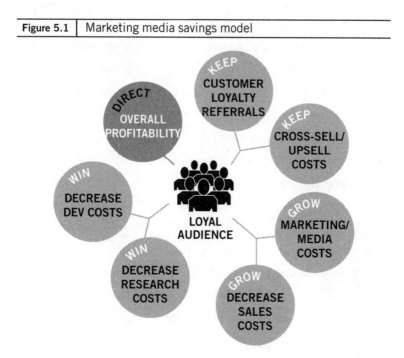

primarily, paid search (such as Google AdWords), events (scanning badges), and thought leadership webinars (accepting registrations).

Like many other technology companies, it utilized content and thought leadership assets to help fuel these paid efforts. Paid traffic from Google ads led to resource and demonstration centers where, in exchange for an email address, prospects could download one or more thought leadership pieces. Name tag scans at conferences were primarily given in exchange for a foam stress ball or a free cappuccino at the company's booth. And webinar registrants were moved into two groups. Those who attended received direct calls from salespeople, and those who didn't received emails inviting them to the resource center.

The challenge was that the company found these approaches were not only becoming more expensive; they were losing their effectiveness. The cost of adding a name into the company's database rose from an average of $15 per name to $18 per name and ultimately to more than $20 per name. Further, the quality of that data was waning quickly. There were more and more false entries such as mickeymouse@gmail.com and other clearly fake ones, providing "data" purely as a means of getting access to the asset.

What the company didn't understand is that this model of marketing will always trend toward a zero-sum game. It will always become harder and harder to reach these people from scratch every time. And what goes unsaid is that many companies end up spending two and three and four times for the very same false information.

Instead, we changed the model. We worked with this company to build a platform, an integrated resource center that provided value to these customers regardless of whether they purchased. Responders weren't considered leads; they were considered an audience. The promotional efforts were used to build "subscribers," not marketing leads.

The company built an audience database—one that it could monetize over time. Many of these audience members aren't ready to buy today, but maybe in a month, or three. The company stabilized its cost per acquisition at around $18 per name. But more importantly, the quality of the data increased exponentially. The company stopped paying for the same false names over and over. These people were providing their high-quality data because they valued the content being delivered consistently. Thus, they provided accurate and rich sets of data to the organization.

Then—and here is the magic—the company also found that once these audiences raised their hands to become leads, they closed twice as often as leads beforehand. So, the company stabilized its cost-per-name acquisition costs and halved its cost-per-customer acquisition costs.

Here's the trick—the company had to be willing to *slow down* its lead-nurturing process. It had to be willing to completely change its approach to sales and marketing. It had to move from building lead databases to building audiences. It went from automatically adding people to its sales funnel to try to persuade them to buy something, and instead to being patient enough to build an audience of people who at some point would volunteer to be put into its sales funnel.

A very different approach—and one that helps save hundreds of thousands of dollars in yearly marketing costs.

Marketing/Media Costs

As the Kraft example makes clear above, the true value of acquiring an audience is the insight that it gives you into how to access and reach the individuals in the audience. Because Kraft delivers value to a loyal audience, the company can utilize the data it gathers to target more accurate and relevant advertising to its potential consumers, and thus it can change the calculus of a traditional digital advertising media buy.

But consider another example: Jyske Bank, the third largest bank in Denmark in terms of market share. As CMI detailed in our documentary *The Story of Content,* Jyske Bank completely transformed how it operated as a marketing department. As its marketers say, the bank is a media company that happens to have its own bank.

They are finding now that it is actually less expensive to become the media than it is to actually try and rent space on it. By creating a 24/7/365 newsroom, the bank has been able not only to develop content that is good enough to build a loyal audience—but it gathers the point that it is getting its content picked up by national Danish television networks. As the editor in chief of the effort, Lasse Hoegledt, has said, "If you can't control the media, you must become the media."

But this approach isn't limited to only those who are spending tens of millions of dollars, or kronor, on traditional media buys. Even small and medium-sized businesses are finding that utilizing subscription data as a means of targeting their advertising can be profitable. One small B2B manufacturer that we worked with is utilizing its renewed audience database as a means of using Google ads more effectively. Once you sign up for its digital magazine, you are tagged with the kind of content you consume. Then, as you surf around, you see relevant advertising through Google's network, targeting you based on your content consumption habits. If you've visited some of the content that is positioned to be a "buy" signal, you might see advertisements that target you as a buyer. If you've visited some of the content that is meant to "inspire" you to change, you will see advertisements meant to draw you in to deeper-level content. This company has already seen a 25 percent effectiveness on its Google ad buy through using this method of marketing.

Cross-Sell and Upsell Costs

OpenText, Canada's largest software company, is a company that develops and sells enterprise information management software. One of the more innovative programs it put in place was a complete media website targeting new clients that were being onboarded. It created a complete library of white papers, checklists, e-books, and case studies welcoming the new clients and continuing to educate them. Through this media site, it created more than 1,700 new contacts at its client companies. This translated into 31 new opportunities worth $1.8 million.

One of the biggest benefits that marketers so rarely realize is how, by actually *slowing down* the process of marketing, by focusing on providing consistent value to your most engaged customers, we can increase the average value of those particular customers. They not only tend to purchase more products, but can also find additional value so that you don't have to discount as much.

Decrease Research and Development Costs

A loyal audience can help save costs by helping to inform the company about what kinds of new products, or new features, the company may want to bring to market. In Chapter 4, Joe told the story of Brian Clark and Copyblogger—the educational resource for online copywriting. One of Brian's biggest secrets to success was his ability to build a loyal audience first and then let the audience inform him of what kind of software might be the most appropriate to sell to his audience. So, rather than spending tons of money developing software that his audience wouldn't be interested in purchasing—he simply listened to the people in his audience tell him all the things they might be interesting in purchasing.

Adobe's CMO.com is a wonderful media platform, with more than 25,000 subscribed senior-level marketers. A huge benefit for Adobe is its ability to look at the content consumption across the CMO.com platform and use that intelligence to understand how it might program its events, its thought leadership programs, and its marketing materials for the kinds of things its senior-level marketer customers might be interested in hearing about.

And as I mentioned in Chapter 1, Johnson & Johnson uses BabyCenter.com as an addition to its research panel of 50,000 consumers with the millions of parents on the website to gain insight from the sentiments shared across the platform.

Among the largest costs in any company are new-product research and development costs. Now, of course, the cost of R&D varies wildly depending on the company and what industry the company is in. A growing software-as-a-service (SaaS) company like Salesforce might spend somewhere between 12 and 15 percent of revenue on new-product development. A pharmaceutical company, on the other hand, lives and breathes R&D and so might spend upward of 20 percent of revenue on R&D. And a car manufacturer like Volkswagen might spend 5 to 8 percent of total revenue on R&D.

But regardless of what percentage, research and development will be a sizable piece of any successful company's business budget. Utilizing a loyal audience to become an ongoing platform of customers to tell you what to make is an asset indeed.

Customer Loyalty and Word-of-Mouth (WOM) Referrals

Looking at how building a loyal, subscribed audience drives loyalty may be my favorite reason for looking at a new way to market through owned media.

Consider a few data points—namely, that despite the huge and in some cases extraordinary efforts of the last 10 years to "know" and "relate to" our customers through data acquisition:

- More than half of U.S. customers switched service providers in the last year due simply to poor customer service experiences—up 5 percent from 2012.

- The rate of loyalty has barely budged among U.S. customers, rising just 1 percent since 2012, and customers' willingness to recommend a company rose by just 2 percent.

- Only 23 percent of consumers say they have any relationship at all with any brand.

- 75 percent of adult Americans say they prefer that their data not be collected or used at all by companies.

A study conducted by the Corporate Executive Board in 2012 concluded that there is no linear correlation between the number of interactions with a customer and the depth of relationship with that customer. Nevertheless, most marketing strategies center on this very metric: the more pushed interactions we have, the more data we glean, then the deeper our relationship must be. It's simply not true.

To the extent that customers are loyal at all, it is to the valuable experience that they continue to have with the brand, and not the product or service that they've purchased.

Now, as we mentioned in Chapter 1, this is where brands and their owned media really began. So the business case here for creating a more loyal customer is one that is relatively easy to make. We can see it working in a number of examples:

- **John Deere's *The Furrow Magazine*.** This brand magazine has been published since 1895 and reaches two million people globally and 570,000 in the United States and Canada. As its current publications manager, David Jones, said, "I've never worked for a brand magazine like this that people loved so much. It is a portal into a brand that people feel passionately about—to the level that kids are wallpapering their rooms with our tractors. You just don't run across that every day."

- *Michelin Guide.* Of course not many people know that the world's fanciest restaurants are graded by a tire company. The Michelin stars that are the most highly coveted rating a restaurant can receive have been given out for more than 100 years. The guide was created so that people would drive more—and thus use more tires.

But truly one of our more favorite examples of generating a profitable loyalty program is the Zappos program we discussed when we sat down with Christa Foley from Zappos. The company's CEO, Tony Hsieh, quite literally wrote the book on loyalty, called *Delivering Happiness*. To say that Zappos is focused on customer service and loyalty is an understatement about both.

Interestingly, Zappos has a profitable way of looking at one part of its loyalty experience. The Zappos Insights program is a revenue-generating method of delivering loyalty-based services. As Christa relayed to us in our interview, it got started quite by accident:

> It was not uncommon, when brand reps would come in to show a product line to our buyers, that we would really welcome them into the office, and we would give them a tour. We've always felt like the more connected you are with customers, our vendors, or really anyone that you work with, that the better partnership you have. So that's how, unofficially, we started giving tours and lessons of loyalty to external people touring in the office.

And now the program is a profitable business unit for the company. As Christa told us:

> It was Tony's idea to try to monetize or leverage that as a potential business opportunity for us. So Zappos Insights was started in 2008 as a small business within zappos.com, and the initial focus was on a membership platform. It's a subscription model within Zappos Insights, where for people who can't come to the office, they can learn about us and learn about how we think about culture and customer service in terms of customer loyalty.

Overall Business Profitability

One of my favorite interviews over the last five years was in 2013 when I interviewed Jonathan Mildenhall, then the head of the Coca-Cola Company's Global Advertising Strategy and Creative Excellence (and now CMO of Airbnb). In talking about Coca-Cola's Content 2020 project, he said:

> But, for the more financially minded of the organization, I say this: If I can fill up the emotional level of the brand, then I have to trade on it less and less. Believe it or not, we're still engaging with new consumers that don't have their emotional well filled.

When I asked him about what "trade on it" meant, he told me that it was, of course, impossible to measure what any one YouTube video, or social post, or infographic contributed to the overall revenue or profitability of Coca-Cola. He said, of course we're going to continue to spend money on paid advertisements. Coca-Cola is one of the largest media buyers on the planet. But more important, he pointed out, is the kind of advertising the company creates. He can drive people to drink more Coca-Cola through discounting it via coupons or "buy one get one free" types of advertising. Or he can "fill the emotional well" through content and get people to pay full price, or even a premium, for the soft drink. He looked at Coca-Cola as a media brand—and his theory was that if he could use a loyal audience of content subscribers that have their emotional well filled, then he would need to discount it (trade on it) less. He could basically affect the entire profitability of the company by using a loyal audience who values the additional experience over the commodity of the product.

When you look, you can see this same strategy is really at the core of Red Bull Media House. By most counts, Red Bull is the most expensive nonalcoholic drink available in any convenience store. And let's be clear: the drink doesn't win many taste tests. In fact, in 2006, the company used to advertise just how bad the product tasted. But through Red Bull Media House, the company has created such a loyal audience through content-driven experiences that customers are more than willing to pay the premium price. And because of the revenue (as Joe mentioned in the previous chapter), Red Bull has, truly, the ability to pivot into any business it likes.

Think about that for a moment. Red Bull's marketing arm is actually enabling the company to sell anything it likes. It already sells high-margin content today. But tomorrow, if Red Bull decided to go into the fashion business, or sell bicycles or surfboards—it could readily do so with loyal customers ready to buy into just about anything the brand wants to bring their way. And they'd be willing to pay a premium price to buy it.

AUDIENCES: THE STRATEGIC SAVINGS ACCOUNT

As we discussed in the beginning of this chapter, our tendency as businesses is to look at the developments of marketing trends with a focus on both hardware and software development. In other words, we look at the development of tablets, or mobile phones, or the Internet of things, or artificial intelligence as yet another platform that we need to account for. Or we see new customer aggregation points, such as broadcast television, cable TV, Facebook, Twitter, LinkedIn, Instagram, or Snapchat as software platforms to which we need to assign special content teams and content strategies.

The result over the last 15 years has been the creation of silos, even within marketing departments. We now have social teams, mobile teams, social CRM teams, e-business teams, web teams, PR teams, brand teams, and on and on.

It's simple: businesses must realize that it is not possible to have a separate silo for every marketing channel on which they must ensure the brand story is being told.

It is vital for marketing departments to stretch and create valuable content across the entirety of the funnel, because that content can (and will) be shared by customers. That's the only way a brand can ever hope to be on as many channels as is necessary. Every valuable experience or piece of content that is shared by audiences across a social network reduces the need of that brand to maintain presence on that channel.

Thus, the *only way to scale* in content is to transform the marketing department's structure and purpose around the creation, management, and ultimate flow of information (i.e., content) to both describe and, more importantly, create value for customers.

And this must happen despite existing or future channels. In short, marketing departments must implement new organizational changes that meet the fast-changing needs of customer empowerment and the need for the organization to orchestrate the vast amounts of content it produces.

The description of value is relatively well understood. There is no doubt that marketing departments are producing exponentially *more* content than ever before to describe the value of their products and services. It's the transformation of marketing into a function that *creates* valuable experiences and content that is the new muscle for most organizations—one we hope to exercise and develop a bit with this book.

So, ultimately these arguments explain why everything must change about how we take our businesses to market. Marketing has to be built in order to create value, not just describe it. We're classically trained as marketers to describe value across the Four Ps. Now, we must do more by creating value using both content and experiences.

As stated before, it's not enough for brands to just act like media companies—they must become media companies that develop and delight audiences continually. As media companies, brands engage customers through every aspect of the marketing funnel:

- From their first awareness of the product, service, or brand promise

- Through their nurturing and decision-making process

- To when they become customers

- To when they become loyal, upsold, cross-sold, and ultimately evangelistic about subscribing to our brand approach

In many companies today, marketing is simply the service organization that views the sales department as a "customer" and exists simply to support sales with the materials the sales staff needs. Even worse, in some companies, marketing is an annoyance that just creates pretty brochures while the "important work" happens elsewhere. In some companies, content, and the creation of it, is seen simply as busywork for the folks in marketing to do when they have no new brochure or ad to create. For many this won't change, and their inaction will be fundamental in their demise.

In this new model of marketing, unique, impactful, differentiating content-driven experiences will become an investment that's every bit as important as product development. One key benefit is that marketing can be the grand savings account for the enterprise. Successful marketers will adapt and change in a constantly evolving media operation that focuses on creating delightful experiences to inform, entertain, engage, and evolve the customer.

Profitable Insights

- In many ways, the features offered in new software are driving our marketing strategy, instead of the other way around. A chase to more and more efficiency using technology is ultimately a zero-sum game. We must find ways to create strategy that is supported with technology. The exponential savings in marketing will come from being able to more easily reach consumers we have a relationship with, not in finding more efficient ways to locate the ones we don't.

- We can decrease sales costs by using content consumption as a means of helping sales have more relevant conversations with consumers.

- We can drive down traditional advertising media costs by using audience data to more accurately target the consumers who are in the market for our products and services.

- We can create better customers, who ultimately buy more products and services from us, by slowing down the process of engagement and better educating them.

- We can decrease product and research costs by developing audiences who willingly tell us what they want from the products and services we put into the marketplace.

- We can increase profitability by looking to media models that develop multiple lines of value at a higher margin than for the business we are currently in.

Profitable Resources

- Scott Brinker, "Only 9% of Marketers Have a Complete, Fully Utilized Martech Stack," Chiefmartec.com, August 20, 2015, http://chiefmartec.com/2015/08/9-marketers -complete-fully-utilized-martech-stack/.

- "15 B2B Case Studies Show How Content Marketing Drives ROI," *NewsCred Insights*, February 24, 2015, https://insights.newscred.com/15-b2b-case-studies-show -how-content-marketing-drives-roi/#sm.0000icw0wm 16zgcvcugveml768xt5.

- Christopher Heine, "Why Johnson & Johnson Treasures BabyCenter's Data," *Adweek*, April 4, 2014, http:// www.adweek.com/digital/why-johnson-johson-treasures -babycenters-data-156720/.

- "U.S. 'Switching Economy' Puts Up to $1.3 Trillion of Revenue Up for Grabs for Companies Offering Superior Customer Experiences, Accenture Research Finds," Accenture.com, October 22, 2013, http://newsroom .accenture.com/news/us-switching-economy-puts-up-to -1-3-trillion-of-revenue-up-for-grabs-for-companies -offering-superior-customer-experiences-accenture -research-finds.htm.

- Karen Freeman, Patrick Spenner, and Anna Bird, "Three Myths About What Customers Want," *Harvard Business Review*, May 23, 2012, http://blogs.hbr.org/2012/05/ three-myths-about-customer-eng/.

- "When Are Consumers OK with Brands' Collecting Personal Data?," MarketingProfs, accessed May 1, 2017, http://www.marketingprofs.com/charts/2014/25456/when-are-consumers-ok-with-brands-collecting-personal-data.

- Christa Foley of Zappos, interview by Claire McDermott, January 2017.

6

First Steps on the Road to Killing Marketing

BY
ROBERT
ROSE

*Don't bend; don't water it down; don't try to make it logical;
don't edit your own soul according to the fashion. Rather,
follow your most intense obsessions mercilessly.*

—Franz Kafka

You can get what you want or you can just get old.

—Billy Joel

So, if we are to reinvent marketing, what are the first steps to making this change?

It probably bears mentioning at this point in our journey that both Joe and I are clear-eyed about the realities of making a switch to the entire function of marketing in our business. This is not something we take lightly, nor do we expect it should or will happen overnight for most businesses.

Our aim is to understand the implications and opportunity of this transformation. As we've stated, one of the biggest mistakes we've made as marketers over the last 17 years is to make small, incremental changes such as digital marketing, social media marketing, content marketing, and other operational models without asking how it might fundamentally change how the business operates.

We believe marketing is transforming from a group that creates its value by simply describing the experience the customer will have with the product or service being offered. Instead, new marketing strategies must lead the entire business strategy, by focusing experiences that deliver value that go well beyond the product or service.

In order to do that, we must take a pragmatic approach to evolve and create new processes that support this change.

THE PROBLEM OF MARKETING'S NONRESPONSE TO CUSTOMER EVOLUTION

As we've discussed, market realities have changed the ways that customers now become aware, browse, investigate, purchase, use, complain, and/or become loyal to a brand. However, the business processes that facilitate awareness, shopping, differentiation, use, and service have not changed. To date, the legacy approach has been to throw teams and technology at all the individual stratifications of the funnel and to create ever more campaign-based efforts to optimize each stratum.

The force of this legacy approach has been strong enough to encourage the service providers and agencies to do exactly the same. Many brands use different agencies for different slices of their business. Even big agencies now have a "direct group" and a "digital group" and an "experiential group" and a "loyalty group." This has significantly reduced the value that agencies are providing to their clients.

Interestingly, and ironically, media companies are evolving faster than marketers here. Big publishers such as the *New York*

Times, Wall Street Journal, Condé Nast, Time Inc., and others all have built branded content studios in order to compete with agencies that still cling to traditional media, banner ads, and 30-second spots. But they aren't stopping there, either. Media companies are quickly moving into product development, offering physical products to accompany their media-centered revenue models.

As Joe detailed in Chapter 3, Dennis Publishing, one of the largest independently owned media companies in the United Kingdom, has now expanded into automobile sales. The media company purchased the online car dealer BuyaCar—which now accounts for 16 percent of Dennis's total revenue.

On the other hand, Marriott has stated that it is "now a media company." It seeks to become the leading lifestyle media brand for travel and leisure. As David Beebe, Marriott's Emmy-winning vice president of global creative, said:

> We hired a lot of media, took a lot of people who were previously storytellers, turned them into marketers. It's all the same thing today. You can't argue with the fact that people aren't engaging with traditional [advertising] and this is the way to do it. You have to try it.

And this—trying it—is the key challenge. Most marketing departments are currently working separately to highlight the company's value by creating more digital experiences than ever before. What must change is the structure of the strategy, to deliver a cohesive, connected, and consistent portfolio of content-driven experiences that evolve marketing into a group that builds loyal audiences, and to integrate everything a brand does (physical or otherwise) to drive a profitable outcome for the business.

To be clear: we propose new, valuable content experiences, which should be created and managed by the marketing team.

They *will be part* of and ultimately enhance the total customer experience. But they will offer separate and distinct value from the product. They should not be created like a campaign, nor as content has always been created, as a response to a new offering, but rather like a product itself.

A great example of this is Cleveland Clinic—an example we discussed earlier. Amanda Todorovich, the director of content marketing for the company, told us about how Cleveland Clinic has completely flipped how it presents content to the leadership in its business. She said:

> One of the interesting conversations that we've been having with leadership, is this whole idea of the business of content. Right? This is going to be something that all content marketing groups will have to think about at some point.
>
> Whether it's the size, scope, and scale of something like what we're doing, or on a smaller, case-by-case basis, marketers are going to have to address this. We have to build in leadership into the business of content that understands the business risks and understands the value of your content is really treating your content as an asset to the entire organization.

In the five years that Joe and I have been working with enterprises of all sizes, we've found that there are three core components that the marketing team needs to have in place to begin this kind of transformation.

THREE CORE COMPONENTS OF THE CHANGE IN PROCESS

Whether achieved through a reinvention of marketing, an evolution (or elevation) of content strategy, or a more focused integration, these three skill sets, or competencies, are common among the companies that are succeeding, and can provide a strong business case for a new process (or approach) to exist to manage it.

They are:

1. **Orchestrating events, not guiding buyers' journeys.**
    Put simply, managing a portfolio of content-driven media experiences is not focused on pulling people through buying paths or journeys. Rather, companies should look to orchestrate a few remarkable events that inspire subscription (building audiences) and a move to the next experience. Regardless of whether it is a long, high-touch B2B journey or a completely transactional B2C journey, customers don't want to be guided; they simply expect to be charmed at every step, and on their own terms. Subscribing to valuable experiences becomes the goal.

2. **Meaning-driven, not data-driven.** Data by its very definition has no meaning. It is simply a collection of facts and statistics aggregated for reference or analysis. To make data meaningful, businesses must develop new strategies to find the emotional value in data that is given, rather than gathered. Instead of looking for "proof of life" within the data, they must instead ask insightful and honest questions and look for the differentiating value—and insight—in *why* the data was provided to begin with.

3. **Organizing for agility, not speed.** Much has been made about the need for marketing departments to be more agile—but it's not necessarily about moving faster. The inability to find the calm out of the chaos, and the constant pressure of "more," is due to a fear of moving too

slowly. Rather, a reinvented marketing team can find joy in the balance of creating strategic, customer-centric experiences that evolve customers and reorienting to more agile strategies.

Let's look at each of these.

1. Orchestrating Events, Not Guiding Buyers' Journeys

A lot of digital ink is spilled on how businesses should map their digital content platforms to the buyer's journey. To be clear, this is still a worthwhile function. What a new marketing team needs to realize, however, is that the map shouldn't be drawn to increase the number of mile markers that guide customers through the brand's ecosystem of marketing and content experiences. The point is, rather, to establish the right *balance* of experiences. The goal, in fact, should be to provide the *least* amount of conversion friction between the customer, the desired action, and the value to the customer's purpose.

Yet because of the ease with which businesses can create and publish new content platforms, marketers have taken the classic lesson of "reach and frequency" to absurd levels in some cases. Every siloed group now maintains its own "content" platforms for its small slice of the buyer's journey. Teams are rewarded for the number of interactions they can create with a customer—with a flawed notion that this drives a deeper relationship between the customer and the business more broadly. In fact, it's usually quite the opposite.

So—in other words—our traditional model of marketing is looking at the products and services we want to sell, and then trying to create "stops" along the buying journey that slow the customers down just long enough to convince them they should purchase it. Instead, can we switch the whole role of media and marketing to that of orchestrating valuable platforms that customers inherently want to be a part of and will subscribe to? Then, within that universe of customers, can we figure out how to develop such trust and insight that they will naturally find the things that we manufacture? In short we *lead*, from the top down, from brand onward with valuable media products that build audiences that inform and provide integrated business value.

The Culture of Content

Casper, a mattress company, is changing the entire way that you will buy bedding. Its marketers utilize Van Winkle's, a stand-alone news and media digital experience that (as Casper says) is part of the company's mission to "own the culture of sleep." The company also operates a blog called *Pillow Talk*, as a way to look more specifically at bedding. And in the spring of 2016, Casper's sleepsleepsleepsleep.com went live—an eight-part series that extolled, in poetic terms, the value of sleep. And Casper's social channels share valuable, fun, and tongue-in-cheek ways to draw in its audiences. It is leading with content and building loyal audiences along the way. And it is spending money on paid media, in large part, to support the content platforms. While search and paid social are big investments, Casper is investing heavily in content amplification platforms such as Outbrain and Taboola to promote earned and owned media. As Philip Krim said in 2015:

> We're proud that we've been able to grow our spend and see CPAs drop and ROI go up even when we're increasing budgets dramatically.

> ### *Key Learning*
>
> *High-performing brands are developing balanced portfolios of digital media experiences that map across the buyer's journey, are integrated across both physical and digital channels, and feature many different content types. These companies structure their owned media portfolios to benefit the customer first and to benefit the delivery mechanism of the content second. Many have created specific cross-functional teams that are organizing both physical and digital content platforms, as well as architecting ways to integrate these experiences together.*

2. Meaning-Driven, Not Data-Driven

As marketers, if CMOs have been chasing any one technology with the help of our CIO colleagues, it's that of using data to optimize our results. Whether we call it data-driven or big data, or, now, machine learning, almost every technology and strategy we've been pushing for is to provide for optimized advertising placement, personalized content, faster iterations of communications to possible customers, and predictive analytics to tell us what to do next.

But here's the thing: this strategy is bumping into a ceiling.

Programmatic, targeted advertising is, quite literally, self-defeating. It's ultimately bad for the advertiser, it's bad for the publisher, and it's bad for the consumer. The whole value of targeted advertising is that it targets a very specific customer of the brand, as opposed to the more general audience. Then, the ad follows that customer around the Internet and pops up on all the sites the brand rents space on. But consider a conversation that Walt Mossberg, executive editor of *The Verge* and former *Wall Street Journal* technology reporter, had with a dinner colleague. Walt said:

I was seated next to the head of this advertising company, who said to me something like, "Well, I really always liked AllThingsD and in your first week I think Recode's produced some really interesting stuff." And I said, "Great, so you're going to advertise there, right? Or place ads there?" And he said, "Well, let me just tell you the truth. We're going to place ads there for a little bit, we're going to drop cookies, we're going to figure out who your readers are, we're going to find out what other websites they go to that are way cheaper than your website and then we're gonna pull our ads from your website and move them there."

Think about that for a second. With programmatic, gone are the days when marketers looked to the prestige and trust of a media property to have alignment with their brand. Now, the calculus is simply how do I get the cheapest click, faster, and personalize it so that I'm ready with my mousetrap when that person is ready to shop.

Surveilling customers across either other publishers or even our own buying channels can provide value, but it is inherently limited. Yes, it makes sense to know how to cross-sell or upsell customers as we watch what they buy or browse. But it only gives us insight into what that customer is interested in, when the customer is interested. What we want is better insight into how to interest that customer to begin with.

And this data is getting harder and harder to get. Consider that in Europe, new rules to protect consumer privacy are already in place. The GDPR (General Data Protection Regulation) is relatively unknown in the United States, but will have sweeping implications over the next 5 to 10 years for any country that's doing business in Europe. While it is more nuanced than this, the basic focus of the GDPR is to curtail data gathering in surveillance-style marketing. Regardless of what happens over the next four to eight years in U.S. politics regarding data and privacy, gathering data on consumers is going to become more complex, not less so.

But as marketers, if we begin to look at data that is given rather than gathered, we can see the value of that data, and the insight it provides, increase exponentially. If we ask ourselves *why* the consumer gave us the data, or we can at least discern that the person willingly gave it to us—it is simply much more valuable to us. Think of the story of Johnson & Johnson's BabyCenter.com and how the valuable data and insight its marketers glean from their customers is freely and willingly provided. It also immediately complies with the GDPR because it is data that is freely given in exchange for value—the media consumed. Perhaps instead of starting with persuasion and hoping to surveil our customers as they browse our shopping aisles, we could start our strategy with value through media—and begin to understand *when* is the most appropriate time to ask them whether they are ready to purchase something.

The Beauty of the Rational and the Emotional

As the roles of the CMO and CIO continue to evolve, the use of content and data to enhance customer experiences is one of the primary drivers of this transformation of the marketing function. But data alone is just a series of meaningless raw numbers that often only distract from the real issues that may be at play. Consider how many times today data is used to measure "proof of life" for a new marketing team or technology that has been put into service. That team has every incentive to manage its performance without regard for, and sometimes even in competition with, the other marketing teams and technologies.

The classic example here is the separation between sales and marketing teams in B2B organizations, where the "digital experience" can be entirely different once the "handoff" is made. But across all types of organizations, it's not uncommon for marketing teams to build walled gardens where data and measurement are held prisoner to the goal of the team.

Data and the digital experience become meaningful when they generate true, actionable insight. In isolation, data contains theoretical answers to problems the business probably doesn't understand. And experiences alone are simply creative projects or performance art. True *meaning* emerges when experiences are infused with the insight and contextual optimization afforded by data. And the infusion comes from creative, insightful questions that are designed to improve the process, not prove the point.

Wilson Raj, who is the global customer intelligence director at SAS, frames this very elegantly when he says, "*Data, while powerful, is only half the story. The other half is an understanding of the emotive needs of our customer. What are their aspirations, fears, dreams, desires etc.?*"

High-performing businesses are balancing both the rational and the emotional to optimize the digital experiences they are creating for customers.

It's important to distinguish between an analytics problem and a data problem. To quote Wilson Raj again:

> CMOs must ask, "do I have the data?" If the answer is "yes," but I can't get at it, I don't have a Big Data problem. I have an analytics problem. But, if the answer is "no," then the CMO must start to examine where they can get it and add in the missing linkages.

This is a critical factor for both the CMO and the CIO. In order to properly ask, "*Do I have the data?*" the business must first know the answer to "*What data is needed?*"

In order for data to have more value for a business than existing information, marketers will need to transform marketing. The focus on using analytics as a method to "prove" success or ROI will not be sustainable. Instead, marketers must use data and measurement to improve the ongoing process of deriving more meaningful insight in order to develop fewer but more beautiful and powerful experiences for customers.

Key Learning

To accomplish this, high-performing businesses will develop new leadership roles on the marketing team. These editorial strategists will be charged with creating initiatives and strategies that peel back the layers of Big Data to make it small, manageable, and most of all meaningful. They aren't necessarily scientists or mathematicians. But they will have the talent to ask advancing questions of data, customers, and influencers. They can then apply the art of listening, conversation, and synthesis to transform facts and results into meaningful insights that move the business forward.

3. Organizing for Agility, Not Speed

Agile is a term that all the marketing kids are dancing to these days. But what often gets lost in translation is the difference between being fast—and being truly agile.

Undoubtedly, the digital disruption has left marketers struggling to rediscover the joy in the practice of marketing. Recent studies have found that more than 66 percent of CMOs feel pressure from their CEO or board to prove that marketing has value. And another 60 percent said those leaders are "turning up the heat."

Moreover, marketers are feeling the pressure of becoming developers of digital media experiences. One study surveyed the Global 1,000 businesses on how they were reorienting their operations to manage the "modern, always-on and mobile shopper" and found that 96 percent of respondents said that integrating digital components has fundamentally affected their business. Sadly, a third of the marketers in these businesses said that these shifts have *"left them feeling 'under pressure and vulnerable.'"*

These are critical observations. High-performing organizations are reorienting their businesses and finding that "more and faster" is the wrong metric and that they must step out of it. The fear of moving too slowly is causing marketers to do foolish things and to develop *more* ads across more social channels and conduct smaller experiments with digital content rather than trying to optimize a set of well-defined media experiences.

This is the difference between quick and fast—and it's how high-performing companies have developed a joyful process with marketing and technology. Their new methodologies help to create and manage customer-centric experiences. As they evolve beyond the old, stale hierarchies and processes of the last 100 years, these companies are changing the way they infuse these experiences intelligently into every part of the customer journey. Put simply: they are reorienting to agile strategies, not fast strategies.

As the number of potential digital experience opportunities explodes, businesses must resist the urge to be everywhere all the time—and instead focus on being in the right place at the right time.

Key Learning

Today's "social conversation" and "real-time" experiences that are being created should not be an unrelenting "Have you heard us yet?" and then three seconds later, "We said, have you heard us yet?" For high-performing organizations, the goal now should

> be a permanent state of agility—of *"We are here when you need us."* In other words, it's not how fast the push notification arrives every time the customer is out for a jog. It's the ability to quickly send the notification of the nearest pharmacy *when asked*, either through an automated preference or when requested explicitly.

Understanding the difference between being agile and moving fast brings the joy back to the process of marketing, and it is one of the key first steps in transforming marketing into a profit-making thinking machine.

REDESIGN MARKETING FOR CREATING CONTENT EXPERIENCES

It's simple: marketers *must* get beyond the cycle of chasing campaign-oriented capabilities around every emerging channel. To succeed, marketing departments must transform.

They certainly must be able to *describe the value* of the product or service for sale through various campaign-focused offline and online content islands such as television, print, social, mobile, or other. But they must also *create differentiated experiential value* that is separate and distinct from that product or service—and then integrate the physical and digital world together seamlessly.

This new focus beyond the campaign requires that content must be made real. Content can no longer be simultaneously everyone's job and no one's job. **The creation, collaboration, management, publishing, and promotion of content-driven experiences must be an actual strategic function in the business.**

To accomplish this, new processes must be created. And then, new roles must be created to facilitate those processes. This is an approach or methodology that focuses on the creation of content-driven experiences as a separate, profitable asset. It has as much potential value as our product and has both revenue and cost-savings possibilities. This is the essence of a new approach to serve this new function we will call marketing.

Profitable Insights

- One of the first steps to evolving marketing to this new model is to stop looking at pulling customers through every step of their "buying journey" and simply create remarkable experiences at selective stops along that journey. If we focus on inspiring customers to subscribe to us and to desire another experience, we are much further along than by persuading them constantly to take another step.

- The use of data must have an emotional component to it. Data has no meaning; it's simply a collection of facts and statistics. But if we look to deriving more emotional data (data that consumers willingly provide), we can take a big step toward making the data we collect so much more valuable.

- We've put too much focus on moving fast. Marketing professionals are already moving at breakneck speed. We need to, instead, focus on creating processes and governance mechanisms that help us move in an agile way, and not always fast. It's about looking to move, adapt, and pivot quickly, rather than always running fast.

Profitable Resources

- Joe Lazauskas, "'We're a Media Company Now': Inside Marriott's Incredible Money-Making Content Studio," Contently.com, November 5, 2015, https://contently.com/strategist/2015/11/05/were-a-media-company-now-inside-marriotts-incredible-money-making-content-studio/.

- Amanda Todorovich of the Cleveland Clinic, interview by Claire McDermott, January 2017.

- Sara Sluis, "Casper the Friendly Online Mattress Startup Experiments Early with New Platforms," AdExchanger .com, February 17, 2015, https://adexchanger.com/advertiser/casper-the-friendly-online-mattress-startup-experiments-early-with-new-platforms/.

- Eric Johnson, "25 Years Later, Walt Mossberg Says Technology Is Still Too Hard to Use," Recode, accessed May 1, 2017, http://www.recode.net/2016/5/9/11636082/ walt-mossberg-code-conference-preview-recode-relaunch.

- MarketingCharts staff, "2 in 3 CMOs Feeling Pressure from the Board to Prove the Value of Marketing," Econsultancy .com, August 29, 2013, http://www.marketingcharts.com/traditional/2-in-3-cmos-feeling-pressure-from-the-board-to-prove-the-value-of-marketing-36293/.

- Christopher Ratcliff, "96% of Enterprise Businesses 'Feeling the Pressure' of Digital Transformation," Econsultancy.com, August 27, 2014, https://econsultancy.com/blog/65351-96-of-enterprise-businesses-feeling-the-pressure-of-digital-transformation#i.19dz5w915ufdf.

7

The One Media Model

BY
JOE
PULIZZI

Words are, in my not-so-humble opinion, our most inexhaustible source of magic. Capable of both inflicting injury, and remedying it.

—J. K. Rowling, *Harry Potter
and the Deathly Hallows*

It is not the beauty of a building you should look at; it's the construction of the foundation that will stand the test of time.

—David Allan Coe

I've been speaking on the topic of content marketing for over 10 years now. During that time, content marketing has become a driving force, maybe *the* biggest change I've seen in the approach to marketing. We are slowly evolving from a product-centric to a more audience-centered strategic approach.

And yet marketers tend to overcomplicate the idea of content marketing. There is still a belief that we need to be everywhere our customers are on the web. That we need to be on all social platforms (like it or not). That we need to be distributing our stories 11 different ways every day. That we need to create viral content (don't get me started on that one).

So when I take the stage telling marketers in the United States, Finland, Germany, Australia, and the United Kingdom to slow down, choose channels carefully, possibly desert publishing on some social media sites, and simplify their strategies, I often get pushback.

"Too simplistic," I hear.

"My management expects us to publish on every platform," I hear again and again.

"We need immediate results" is a common theme.

All I can say is, you should zig when everyone else is zagging.

Let your competitors waste their time and resources publishing more and more content, while you go out and build a loyal audience that will reap rewards for years to come.

Remember, more content does not mean more assets. The asset is the audience, and the content is what gets you to the asset. Once you develop the asset that is the audience, then (and only then) can you drive revenues and profits.

As Robert always says, "Our goal is not to create more content. It's to create the minimum amount of content with the maximum amount of resources."

A SIMPLIFIED APPROACH

Once an enterprise of any size decides to begin creating content, the inclination is to start as soon as possible. But first we need to make sure that we have a proper hypothesis for doing so, and that any content we create makes sense for our audience (or future audience) and our business.

Following are the questions you need to answer as you proceed into any marketing approach, but will be particularly helpful for a content-as-business-model approach.

Big-Picture Questions

These are broad questions that must be answered in order to start your documented strategy.

1. **What is the challenge?** What business challenge (specifically) are you trying to solve?

2. **The ultimate outcome.** What is your dream outcome of this approach?

3. **The risk.** What is the risk if you fail?

4. **Who's involved?** What permission do you need from your managers to participate?

5. **The budget.** How much will you spend on this approach?

6. **What if things go wrong?** What is your plan if you don't achieve your goals quickly enough, if there is a customer complaint, or if other problems arise?

7. **Time.** How long do you have to show success?

These are broad questions for a reason: they are intended to get you into the right mindset before you start to talk about any type of content creation.

Getting More Specific

1. What's the specific need to reach the objective? Create leads, better customers, higher-quality leads, direct sales, etc.?

2. How big an opportunity is it? Is this opportunity big enough to warrant spending your time and/or money on?

3. How will the initiative align to your business objectives? With your existing marketing?

4. What are the risks? Identify the sources of risk on achieving the goals you've set. Focus on the things you can control, and identify what you can do to minimize the possibility of these things occurring.

Audience Questions

Now that you have a feel for the problem you are trying to solve and the reason to create content in the first place, you can begin to focus on the persona.

1. Who's the target audience? (There can be only one.)

2. What's the audience's content or informational need or needs as it pertains to this plan?

3. How will this help the people in your audience with their job or life in some way?

4. Why does the audience care about this? (Do the people care?)

5. What unique value proposition (UVP) do you offer this persona? What differentiating value do you bring to the table?

Content Questions

You want to highly scrutinize the content. If the information isn't truly differentiated, with limited competition, there is very little chance you will break through and gather attention.

1. What is the content niche you are planning to cover?

2. What other companies are providing this kind of information? Do you even have an opportunity to become a leading resource in this area? How do you find out?

3. Is there a possibility to purchase an existing external asset instead of developing a new one?

4. Where will these stories be found? Who in the company has the expertise to help? What internal assets and other content do you have already?

5. What resources (staffing and otherwise) do you not have that you will need?

6. How will the stories mainly be told (audio, video, textual)? Remember, you want to focus on one key content type and one key distribution platform (a blog, a magazine, an event series, a podcast, a video series, etc.).

7. What key design issues will make or break the program?

8. What platform makes the most sense to distribute the content?

9. Are you creating a new content brand, or are you weaving into your existing product or company brand?

Distribution and Measurement

1. How will the information be found by the audience?

2. What current assets do you have to distribute the content? What partnerships can be leveraged? Is there paid budget available?

3. How will you know the initiative is successful?

4. What subscription tools will you use to capture audience information?

5. What key assets need to be created in order to capture the necessary data?

6. What other departments should you bring in to maximize impact?

7. What technology are you missing to enable collaboration and measurement? What are "must-haves" and what are "nice-to-haves"?

8. What internal communication will you need to make sure the program gets and keeps buy-in?

9. How quickly, considering the buying cycle, can you tie the initiative to sales, cost savings, or customer loyalty?

10. What internal issues need to be worked out so you can tie the subscribers to revenue?

CREATING THE BUSINESS STATEMENT

While there are more questions to be asked, answering the above will uncover the opportunities and gaps in your overall plan.

Now, you'll want to take this information and create a business statement, which will serve as an elevator pitch for the overall project. Here's an example.

Problem: The mechanical engineers (our key buyers and key leads) we are currently gathering from our traditional marketing processes are often coming to us very late in the buyer's journey. This means that even if the sales team can break through and get a meeting, we are trying to win the business solely on price and not on value. Thus, yield has been significantly impacted over the past 12 months. It has become a significant management concern.

Solution: We believe that if we can build a loyal audience of mechanical engineers, developing a remarkable awareness experience for our brand, that we will be able to bypass the RFP process, increase the quality of our leads (pull leads from the subscriber base), and earn more business without competition (and not discounting our product).

Our own engineers are some of the smartest around designing industrial soldering equipment (ISE). Currently, there are three publications that cover the design/build process of ISE, but none solely focus on ISE. We believe, if done right, we can become the leading informational resource in this area, build a loyal subscriber base of mechanical engineers who design/build in this area, and then build our lead flow from the subscriber base after a series of behaviors take place and we hit the appropriate lead score (subscribe, engage, download, attend webinar, etc.).

After reviewing all possible content creation avenues, we believe that a blog/e-newsletter combo would be the most appropriate. The initial plan is to create two blog posts per week (Tuesday and Thursday with a Saturday e-newsletter) until we see a minimum of 5,000 subscribers to the e-newsletter. Once achieved, we will increase velocity to three times per week.

The incentive to sign up for the newsletter will be a free sample template for the design/build process. This has already been developed internally by another department, and we have the department's approval to redesign and share it out (it's an extremely valuable download).

We believe that the 5,000 subscriber mark is achievable in six month's time with adequate promotion leveraging our current database and partnering with outside media organizations. With a buying journey of six months, we believe that we'll start to see yield impact at about the eight-month mark of the program, with the ultimate goal to increase average yield per sale by 15 percent. Considering the budget and resources needed for this program, we believe that between new business and the overall yield impact, the program will generate 5.5x ROI in a 12-month period.

What you just read is the kind of one-page report you would present to your management team. In this case, the goal is only to get your strategic thoughts on paper so that you have a solid business plan and hypothesis for moving forward with this opportunity.

This plan is not set in stone—it can and should change and be updated on a regular basis.

THE LONELY MODEL

ESPN, which originally started as a sports-only cable television station in 1979, began with a $9,000 investment by Bill and Scott Rasmussen. Almost 40 years later, ESPN is the world's most valuable sports media brand, valued at $17 billion according to Forbes.

For 13 years, ESPN directed all its attention to just one channel: cable television. Then in the nineties, the company began to rapidly diversify. It launched ESPN radio in 1992, ESPN.com in 1995, and *ESPN the Magazine* in 1998.

Today, ESPN has a presence on almost every channel and in every format available on the planet—from Twitter and Snapchat to podcasts and documentaries. Yet ESPN didn't diversify until its core platform (cable television) was successful.

The greatest media entities of all time selected one primary channel in which to build their platform:

- *Wall Street Journal*—printed newspaper

- *Fast Company*—printed magazine

- TED Talks—in-person events

- *BuzzFeed*—online magazine format

- Rush Limbaugh—radio show

Most organizations that run to create and distribute more content try to publish as much as they can, in as many different ways, on as many platforms as possible. This is a failing proposition. Frankly, if you are a historian of media companies, you know this just doesn't work.

THE "ONE" MEDIA STRATEGY

In 2014, while I was researching for my book *Content Inc.*, our team of researchers looked at more than 100 successful media brands, as well as content marketing examples. To our surprise, every one followed the exact same model.

Each platform creation had four key attributes:

- One key audience target

- One mission (tilt)

- (Primarily) one content type (audio, video, textual/image, face-to-face)

- One platform (blog/website, iTunes, YouTube, Snapchat, etc.)

Even the *Huffington Post*, which was sold to AOL (now Verizon) for $315 million, didn't start with the hundreds of blogs to hundreds of different audiences and 4,000 contributors. It started with one blog and one (left-leaning) mission.

ONE AUDIENCE AND ONE MISSION

Besides the underlying business model (how the money comes in), there is one thing that media companies do with their content planning that non-media companies do not do.

It's the creation of an editorial mission statement. Media companies start their strategies by developing an editorial mission statement that guides their content creation efforts and serves as a beacon for the overall business. I've launched over 40 media products in my career, from magazines to newsletters to events to webinar programs. In every one of those launches, the first few days were spent creating and fine-tuning the editorial mission. It is simply the first step in establishing a successful strategy.

The Content Mission

A mission statement is a company's reason for existence. It's why the organization does what it does. For example, Southwest

Airlines' mission statement is to democratize the travel experience. The mission statement for CVS is to be the easiest pharmacy retailer for customers to use. So, in simple terms, the mission statement answers the question, "Why do we exist?"

So, in essence, your mission statement needs to define who the specific audience is and why you are creating all this content.

In *Epic Content Marketing*, I discuss three parts of the content mission statement:

- The core target audience

- The material that will be delivered to the audience

- The outcome for the audience

Under the Hood: Digital Photography School

Darren Rowse built two amazingly successful businesses leveraging content as the business model. The first one, ProBlogger, focuses on small business blogging. The second, Digital Photography School, is one of the leading sources for beginning photographers on how to get the maximum out of their picture-taking skills.

But it didn't start out that way. Initially, Darren launched a camera review–type blog. As he explains:

> Previous to ProBlogger I started a camera review blog that was my first commercial sort of blog and that had gotten to the point where it was fulltime, but it wasn't a very satisfying blog to write. My readers would come for one day to research a certain camera and then disappear and never come back. So I always had this dissatisfaction with it that I wasn't actually building a community; I think that's what really feeds me, having ongoing readers. I always wanted a blog that was a bit more about helping people in a long-term way.

After this initial experiment didn't quite work, Darren came back to photography blogging, but he changed his focus (what we call a content tilt). Darren's "aha!" moment came with his focus on one particular audience.

"I guess one of the doubts I had along the way was around focus," says Darren. He recalls:

> Very much early on it was about beginners, so it was very basic content and I had some doubts about whether I should start expanding into more intermediate level content, but I kind of stuck to that beginner stuff for the first two years and really built the audience there until my audience began to grow into the next level of content. So I didn't expand the expertise too early, which was good in hindsight.

That decision paid off, and Darren saw his total email and social audience grow to well over a million subscribers.

Let's take a look at Digital Photography School's content mission: "Welcome to Digital Photography School—a website with simple tips to help digital camera owners get the most out of their cameras."

Let's dissect the mission statement:

- The core target audience: digital camera owners
- The material that will be delivered to the audience: simple tips
- The outcome for this audience of camera owners: get the most out of their cameras

The Content Tilt

As I explained in *Content Inc.*, the content tilt is more than just telling a different story. It's also about **finding an educational or**

informational area of little to no competition where you actually have a chance to break through all the clutter.

In thinking about Digital Photography School, with thousands of websites available that talk about photography, how did Darren break through with little to no promotional budget?

Darren believed that the majority of photography content on the web was (1) focused on the photography professional or (2) in a long textual form that was hard to engage in. Darren's content tilt, the way he separated himself, was his insight and ability to turn his focus on a beginner audience with helpful, consistent tips that his readers could use easily and immediately.

Where Enterprises Go Wrong

CMI consulted with one large technology company that was having trouble with its blog. Specifically, traffic and conversions were steadily retreating for over six months, and the editorial team couldn't identify the problem.

It only took a few minutes into our first meeting to identify the problem.

The editorial team stated that the blog tried to attract up to a dozen different audiences (the buyer personas). What we quickly determined is that in order to create content that was somewhat relevant to each audience, the editorial team had to water down the content. This created a content experience that could be found just about anywhere on the web.

The short story is that this company was not creating anything truly differentiated or meaningful because it was trying to target too many audiences at once.

The greatest media companies target one audience at a time. Anything more and there is no hope to be relevant enough to cut through all the clutter.

Leaning into the Tilt by Getting Uncomfortable

I loved the book *Tools of Titans* by Tim Ferriss.

One of the sections in the book is on James Altucher, former hedge fund manager and many-times-over entrepreneur. In a very short amount of time, James has been able to grow his audience faster than almost anyone else on the web. How? Here it is straight from James: "We all have, let's say, two or three dozen massive pain points that everyone can relate to. I try to basically write about those, and then I try to write about how I attempted to recover from them."

Tim Ferriss goes on to say that he's followed James's advice by asking himself, "What am I embarrassed to be struggling with? And what am I doing about it?"

Let's be honest—this is incredibly difficult for brands of any size to do with their content creation and storytelling, but *it is* necessary. Just answering customer questions and covering the basics of your industry niche are table stakes. You need to differentiate your content in some way.

Over and over as Robert and I visit brands around the world, we find the content they are creating is not special at all. Frankly, it's been done. It's safe content. As Seth Godin says, "We cannot out-obedience the competition." Same begets more same, and you've just wasted everyone's time, both your company's time and the time of whatever audience you have left.

This is exactly how you need to think when deciding on your content tilt. Now is the perfect time to go and analyze your content niche, the editorial mission within that niche, and whether or not you are hitting the mark of differentiated content. If you are like most companies, you probably aren't.

We need to do what Altucher says—really go into the pain points of your audience, whether they are engineers or entrepreneurs. If you don't know what the pain points are, talk to your audience. Talk to your sales reps. Talk to your customer service. The data is available, but perhaps we haven't reached for it yet.

You have the opportunity to do what most companies are scared to do: really talk about the pain around your content in an authentic and maybe even embarrassing way. You shouldn't feel completely comfortable with your content. It should make you squirm . . . just a bit. If it does, you are starting to hit close to home.

Discovering a Content Tilt

Let's go back to the launch of Content Marketing Institute in 2010. Even though I had used the term *content marketing* on and off for the previous nine years, it was still new marketing terminology.

The dominant industry term at the time was *custom publishing*. From conversations with senior marketing practitioners (CMI's target audience), I could tell that that term was not something that resonated with them. But was there an opportunity for content marketing? Could changing the industry terminology be our content tilt?

I tinkered with the Google Trends tool and looked at a number of phrase variations. Here is what I found as it related to the dominant industry term (*custom publishing*) and the emerging term (*content marketing*).

- **Custom publishing.** If this were a stock for purchase, we at CMI definitely wouldn't want to own it. Every year people searched for this term less often. In addition, many of the articles referred, not to our idea of brands creating content, but to customized print books. This confusion was a problem.

■ **Content marketing.** The term didn't even register on Google Trends. I began to think that if enough of the right content was created, a movement around the term could be started. With confusion around the other terms such as *branded content* and *custom content*, it was likely that the industry needed a new term around which to rally key thought leaders. In addition, without a clear leader in the "content marketing" group, CMI could move quickly and gain search market share if done correctly.

So a combination of talking to our audience and using free tools like Google Trends helped CMI define its content niche and "tilt" around this name change. Today, *content marketing* is a recognized industry term and helped CMI become one of the fastest-growing media companies in the world.

HubSpot, the extremely successful marketing automation enterprise, employed the same strategy with the term *inbound marketing*. In 2006, HubSpot launched a blog around the concept and developed a book (called *Inbound Marketing*), a video series, and an event called Inbound. As you can see, the community gathered around this term and helped thrust HubSpot into a leadership position.

One Content Type

According to the 2017 Content Marketing Institute/ MarketingProfs Content Marketing Benchmark Study, the most popular content types are as follows (in order of usage):

■ Articles or blog posts

■ Textual stories in e-newsletters

- Videos

- In-person events

- Reports or white papers

- Webinars/webcasts

- Books (print or digital)

- Printed magazines

- Audio programming

- Printed newsletters

The majority of media success stories fall into the following content types:

- **Articles or blogs (or content-based websites).** CMI's main platform for building audience is by distributing content via a blog. Blogs started at three times per week and now run every day or multiple times per day (including weekends).

- **E-newsletter programs.** *Lenny*, cocreated by *Girls* star Lena Dunham, has over 500,000 e-newsletter subscribers, of which 70 percent open each newsletter.

- **Videos.** Every week, Matthew Patrick of Game Theory distributes a fresh video via YouTube.

- **Podcasts.** Every day, John Lee Dumas (*Entrepreneur on Fire*) presents a new podcast interview.

In each of the above examples, the organizations have grown and diversified into other media products, like magazines, other video channels, podcasts, and more. But each one started out focusing on one key content type first.

One Platform

Now that you know how you are going to tell your story (the content type), you need to decide how you are going to deliver the content—the channel. Over the long term, you'll be distributing your content through a number of channels, but right now you need to make a decision about the "core" channel.

You need to consider two major questions when making this decision:

- What channel offers the best opportunity to reach your target audience? (Reach)

- What channel gives you the most control over presenting your content and building your audience? (Control)

Brian Clark's Copyblogger has almost infinite control over its channel, a WordPress site that it owns. At the same time, Copyblogger needs to build a system to attract people to its content since its website doesn't reside within another ecosystem that can naturally bring it traffic.

On the other hand, the *Entrepreneur on Fire* (EOF) podcast and Game Theory videos have a greater reach possibility than Copyblogger since they publish within an environment with a built-in audience. *EOF* publishes via iTunes, where there are millions of people who search for new podcasts every day. Same thing for Game Theory. Its target audience of teenagers is already on YouTube every day. As long as Game Theory continues to create compelling content that YouTube will deliver, it should grow an audience there.

The problem with *EOF* and Game Theory is that they are leveraging platforms that they have little or no control over. Game Theory has over 8 million subscribers. That's amazing, but technically Game Theory doesn't control those subscriber relationships; YouTube does. YouTube could decide tomorrow that it doesn't want Game Theory to have access to those people, or it might decide to publicize other content, like Jimmy Fallon, to Matthew Patrick's audience instead of Game Theory.

Consider the example of the duo Smosh, the YouTube sensations who built an audience of over 20 million subscribers on YouTube. Over the past couple of years, calls to action at the end of their video content were to their owned website, Smosh.com, where they could sign up people for an email subscription program that they had control over. The point here is if you choose a low-control channel as the main driver of your content distribution, be aware that at some point you'll want to convert the subscribers on that platform to your own subscribers.

What About Social Media?

Although social channels, such as YouTube, Snapchat, and LinkedIn, could be great places to build your digital footprint and followers, you ultimately have no control over what those companies do with your connections. Sure, LinkedIn lets your current connections see all the content you publish on LinkedIn, but LinkedIn could change its mind tomorrow. It has every right to do so as a private business, and you, a free member of the LinkedIn community, have no rights.

Social channels like Facebook, Twitter, LinkedIn, Pinterest, and Instagram and newer channels like Snapchat and Medium may all be solid considerations to build a platform depending on whom you are targeting, but it's important to understand the dangers.

Look at the fastest-growing media companies of today, such as BuzzFeed or Vice. You can even look at a traditional publisher like the *New York Times* or *Time* magazine. They are all very good at leveraging social channels and building an audience on those channels, but they don't build their main platform on social channels.

In every case, they build websites or print properties (both with subscribers) that they can own and control, and they leverage other channels to drive people back to the sites they own so they can convert passersby into an audience they can monetize.

YOUR BEST CHANCE AT REVENUE

I spent the early part of my career in business-to-business publishing. The metric that dominated each publication on which I ever worked was the subscriber. Originally called circulation development, and now audience development, no revenue (the big *z-e-r-o*) was possible without a targeted group of buyers who subscribed to one or many content offerings the media brand provided.

Think about that: **without subscribers, revenue was absent**. That is media yesterday, today, and tomorrow. Look at the leading trade publication in your industry, or check out ESPN, the *Wall Street Journal*, or the *New York Times*. None of them can function without subscribers.

Brian Clark of Copyblogger Media went from "just a blog" to becoming one of the fastest SaaS companies on the planet. The key to his success? Over 200,000 targeted subscribers who know, like, and trust Copyblogger so much that they end up buying just about anything Brian puts in front of them.

While larger enterprises are fighting silo battles, have become embroiled in politics, and are tearing each other apart focusing on (sometimes) meaningless metrics, **those enterprises with patience and passion are building audiences and winning**. Once you build an audience, anything is possible . . . and the subscriber makes it all happen.

THE SUBSCRIBER HIERARCHY

As you analyze your digital footprint and begin to build your audience, your focus needs to be at the top of this hierarchy (Figure 7.1). Simply put, all subscribers are not created equal. If you have a choice, email subscribers are the most valuable ultimately because of control.

Figure 7.1	While all connections can be a good thing, not all connections are equal in value.

Email Subscribers
Print Subscribers
Medium Followers
Twitter Subscribers
LinkedIn Connections
iTunes Subscribers
Snapchat Followers
Pinterest Subscribers
YouTube Subscribers
Facebook/Instagram Fans

■ **Email subscribers.** They allow you the most control and easiest access. Extremely helpful and relevant emails will break through the clutter.

■ **Print subscribers.** You have an incredible amount of control. Communication is never instantaneous, and feedback is difficult. There are cost challenges due to print and postal charges.

■ **Medium followers.** Medium is evolving into more of a content management system, like WordPress. Because of this, Medium allows the publisher certain controls over audience data.

■ **Twitter followers.** You have full control over what you send to followers, but messages have an eight-second lifespan, so it may be challenging to reach the audience regularly.

■ **LinkedIn connections.** More and more, LinkedIn has been changing its algorithm and only showing you certain feed updates.

■ **iTunes subscribers.** Here you have full control over the delivery of audio content, but iTunes doesn't give you access to who subscribes to your content.

■ **Snapchat fans.** One of the best opportunities to build a loyal audience, but the platform is new and Snapchat is just now figuring out how to monetize its platform. Posts don't save, so consistent, new content creation is a must.

■ **Pinterest subscribers.** Pinterest offers full control over delivery of content. Users will see your content if they choose to. There is no ultimate ownership over the platform.

- **YouTube subscribers.** You have some control over content, but YouTube can decide to hold some of your content back if subscribers aren't engaging with your content (called "subscriber burn").

- **Facebook/Instagram fans.** Facebook continually modifies its algorithm, which is out of your control. Fans may or may not see your content depending on this algorithm, although quality, helpful, and interesting content has the best chance of breaking through. Promotional content is almost always shut down by Facebook.

While you have more control with certain subscription options, Jeff Rohrs, chief marketing officer at Yext and author of *Audience*, is adamant that no company "owns" its audience: "The reason that the audience is in different places is that no audience is owned. Regardless of whether you're a major television network, pop star, or professional sports team with rabid fans, you simply do not own your audience. They can get up and leave—mentally or physically—at any time."

This is exactly the reason that amazingly helpful and relevant content is the only way to keep our audience connected to us, regardless of which subscription options we choose to leverage.

One thing is clear: if email is this important to this model (and it is), then you must have an email newsletter worth subscribing to. For example, BuzzFeed gained its popularity due to social sharing on Facebook and Twitter. As Facebook started to change its algorithm, fewer and fewer of BuzzFeed's followers saw its posts. This began to impact BuzzFeed's web traffic numbers. To combat this, BuzzFeed has doubled down on building email subscribers and added more than one million opt-in email subscribers in 2015.

For the media marketing model we are proposing in this book, email is the absolutely best way to monetize your audience. For

CMI, 79 percent of our audience subscribes to our e-newsletter *before* they purchase anything from us. Simply put: build a relationship with the audience first (through email), and then you have the opportunity to monetize that audience.

Is Your E-newsletter Valuable?

In our Content Marketing Institute/MarketingProfs research, over 80 percent of business marketers have an e-newsletter. Of those, almost three of four use their e-newsletter as their main call to action around their blogs, articles, and videos.

I'm an e-newsletter fanatic. I believe they are critical to most any substantial content marketing approach. This is why I cover e-newsletters so much in my speeches. In the past year, I've asked this question approximately 20 times to various marketing audiences: "Is your newsletter really, truly valuable to your target audience?"

Do you know how many have raised their hands in the affirmative? Twelve. (I keep track because it's such a small number.) Just 12 of thousands believe they are delivering their customers a valuable experience via email.

If that's true (which I believe it is), can you imagine how much of our audience's time, as well as our staff's time, we are wasting? It's become a little like social media . . . since email messages are so easy to send and, theoretically, so cheap, we don't spend a lot of time on their creation. We've become part of the clutter problem, not the solution.

With social media platforms becoming pay-to-play, we can't afford to do email wrong any longer.

Here are three considerations for a remarkable email newsletter:

- **Consistent.** Every great e-newsletter is sent at the same time, each day/week/month. That means if you send your email newsletter at 10 a.m. ET on Wednesday, you send it at 10 a.m. ET every Wednesday until the data tells you to change it. Not 10:01. Not 9:59. 10:00. Since the dawn of time, the mark of great media companies has been, and will always be, the consistent delivery of something valuable. Create the expectation of a truly amazing content experience.

- **Truly valuable.** Are you delivering information that is critical to your target audience? You know, the stuff your followers can't live without. I'm not talking about coupons or discounts; I'm talking about real insight that is going to help your customers live better lives or get better jobs.

- **Exclusive.** Are you piling up resource content, or links from your blog, and just putting it into your e-newsletter to send? Is there really something different that only comes in this wonderful e-mail newsletter package?

    See, that's not so bad. CVE—consistent, valuable, and exclusive. That's really all it takes.

    Now take a look at your e-newsletter. How many of the three did you get right?

Robert and I are hopeful that this simplified model is a breath of fresh air. Building an audience takes time, energy, and commitment, so the last thing you need is to be creating a lot of unnecessary content on a hundred different channels.

Profitable Insights

- Before you start to create and distribute content, you need to make sure you have the right strategy first. Creating a hypothesis and sharing that with your team is critical as a first step.

- The greatest media companies of all time started by focusing on one core audience leveraging one main platform.

- Subscribers and connections are not created equal. Even though social media connections can be valuable, they should not be considered as valuable as email or print subscribers where you have more control over the data.

Profitable Resources

- James Andrew Miller and Tom Shales, *Those Guys Have All the Fun: Inside the World of ESPN* (Little, Brown & Company, 2011).

- Darren Rowse, interview by Clare McDermott, February 2015.

- "About Digital Photography School," accessed May 25, 2017, https://digital-photography-school.com/about -digital-photography-school/.

- Jordan Valinsky, "With a 70 Percent Open Rate, Lenny Letter Looks to Video and Beyond," digiday.com, June 16, 2016, https://digiday.com/media/lenny-letter-expansion -plans/.

- *Wikipedia*, s.v. "HuffPost," accessed May 25, 2017, https://en.wikipedia.org/wiki/HuffPost.

- "How Did BuzzFeed Harvest One Million Email Subscribers?," Wildcard Digital via slideshare.net, accessed May 25, 2017, https://www.slideshare.net/wildcard -digital/how-did-buzzfeed-harvest-1-million-subscribers.

- Brian Clark, interviews by Clare McDermott, January 2015, and by Joe Pulizzi, February 2017.

CHAPTER 8

Today: The Beginning

BY
JOE
PULIZZI

Buy land, they're not making it anymore.

—Mark Twain

*If you try to do something and fail, you are vastly better off
than if you had tried nothing and succeeded.*

—Anonymous

Success at this new marketing approach doesn't happen overnight.

The Cleveland Clinic, one of the largest hospital networks in
the world, started its content journey like most other enterprises—
one publication at a time. After years of adding targeted magazines
to different buying groups (for example, a number of patient magazines), it made the decision to create a true content destination.

That destination, called Cleveland Clinic's Health Hub, is
one of the leading resources in the world on patient issues, and it
attracts more than four million consumers per month.

Amanda Todorovich leads the media arm at Cleveland Clinic. The sidebar "Starting the Program" reveals her story in her own words.

Starting the Program

The Cleveland Clinic over the last several years has scaled our content marketing efforts to the point where we are generating significant revenue. One of the first ways that we started doing this, even as long as four years ago, was through syndication partnerships and having other publishers and brands pay us to utilize our content to place on their sites.

And that continues to be a source of revenue over the years that's grown substantially. But in 2016, because our audience grew so large, we launched a partnership on our health essentials blog with another publisher who's managing advertising for us. We tested this prior to signing the contract with our partner by placing Google ads on the site; seeing how much revenue could we generate on our own and whether or not we needed a full-time person to manage advertising sales.

When we started the testing process, it was low risk because with Google we could turn it off any time we wanted. We weren't committed to any time period and so it really helped us understand the ins and outs, the questions that we would be faced with and the things that we weren't able to manage on our own. While we were doing that we also had our agency and consultant to help guide us and point us down this path of choosing a partner, and helped us evaluate some of the proposals we were getting from potential partners.

The team we had in place is really focused on producing amazing content and serving our health consumers. We didn't have a sales staff. We don't have people here who are dedicated to advertising sales. We were curious how much revenue could we actually generate from this.

Focusing on monetization was a big change. So we tested. It was generating a little bit of money, which was nice, but we definitely knew there was potential to do more. So then we launched a full advertising program and generated a large sum of revenue.

In 2017 we have expanded that relationship to include not only our consumer blog but also our physician-targeted blog, and we will double revenue this year.

Selling the Program Internally

When you're a brand there's the risk of feeling like you're endorsing the advertiser or that there are some sort of relationship between our organization and theirs. We had to do a lot of due diligence in terms of what our advertising policy would say and what kind of categories we would block. There are certain things as an academic medical center and nonprofit organization we were not allowed to do.

We had many conversations with our legal team and our PR team to understand the reputational risks and what we wanted to do, poring over all of the different categories that we would allow and not allow.

This did not change our editorial approach. This was considered a bonus to what we were already doing because we launched our content marketing efforts to generate brand awareness and national reputation. That was still the number one goal.

We've been producing three to five posts a day on the consumer blogs for several years. We weren't looking to increase that dramatically or put in more resources. We wanted to stick *with what we were doing, but at the same time drive revenues. We believed we could do that through our editorial approach of providing useful, helpful, and relevant content to our audience. Sticking to that was crucial. Getting buy-in and support up front made a big difference.*

Success Factors

We take the revenue that we generate and reinvest it back into content creation. This allows us to continue to grow our audiences, and support our goals of brand awareness and reputation building, which will then help us drive more revenue.

This model is a risk for any organization. Once you start to do something like this and bring revenue into an organization in a way that was never anticipated, people start to pay attention. They start to ask "how can we do more?"

We are successful because of our commitment to an editorial approach. I think where it gets risky as a brand is you may get greedy and do things to compromise the true mission for more revenues. That's where we've been really strong in making sure that that doesn't happen.

This begged the question of how else can marketing generate revenue? When you start to operate like a media company within an organization you then see all the other ways media companies make money. We are now looking at events, special issues, and so many more things we never used to. Why wouldn't we?

If there wasn't trust in marketing's performance and judgment this would have never been a possibility. Because the risks are there. But understanding them, communicating them, and proving that we're sticking to our mission and that the content we're producing is always serving the best interest of our organi-

zation. We would not have been successful if we didn't build that credibility first within the executive team.

Looking Back

When we first started having these conversations with partners, we built the contracts with traffic thresholds that were where we were at the time. Without adding any more resources or developing more content, we continued to grow traffic and revenue. Simply put, great content does great things for any brand.

We've been extremely blessed by what's come of all of our hard work but the strategy, the approach, that commitment, that consistency of great content that serves our audiences must provide value to them every day. **And you cannot generate revenue with content unless it does those things for people**.

Growing the Program

Acquisition [acquiring outside web properties] has not been a part of our game plan. But, I would say as we look ahead it's about how can we continue to think like media, think like a publisher, but still being true to our brand and who we are. We have still more of our own digital content, digital properties that we have potential to generate more revenue opportunities. So it's about exploring that. It's about looking across our enterprise and making sure that anybody who's publishing anything under our name is following the best practices that we've established, really understanding what works and what doesn't, leveraging the data we have both from our own analysis as well as the things that our partners are bringing to the table.

Our partner isn't just selling advertising. They are a publisher themselves and so they have great resources for us that have *been extremely valuable in helping us decide what to do next to our sites to make them better, or where to invest in creating more content, or what possibilities there might be across our properties. It's about how can we leverage what we're learning as we go and continue to evolve.*

One of the interesting conversations that I've been having with leadership is the idea of the business of content. That's the role that content and marketing departments are going to have to be thinking about.

Whether it's to the size, scope, and scale of something like what we're doing or on a small case-by-case basis, the organization needs someone who understands the business risks and understands the value of your content, and is treating your content as an asset to the entire organization. Businesses that make the decision to go in this direction must formalize that decision-making process and be smart about how they're utilizing content for the business.

Advice to Organizations

Find a way to test it. Find a way to have a case study or pilot program. Find a low risk entry point and do something that helps you determine if it's the right direction to go in. Ask your stakeholders. Test it with your audience and see what you get because it's hard to make decisions like this without any data, without any insight from your specific instance. Having that data is what allowed us to do this at scale and continue in our current direction.

MINIMUM VIABLE AUDIENCE

Eric Ries, in his book *The Lean Startup*, talks about the concept of the minimum viable product (MVP). According to Ries, the MVP is a "version of a new product which allows a team to collect the maximum amount of validated learning about customers with the least effort."

The concept is simple: build the minimum product possible, find out if people will pay for it, and use the customer feedback to keep iterating and building a better product.

The same concept can be used for your media marketing model, but in this case, it would be a minimum viable audience (MVA). Brian Clark, founder of Copyblogger, began using this term in 2012. Brian believes that Copyblogger's success (it's never launched a product or service that failed) is due to building a minimum viable audience.

Clark states that an MVA has three components:

1. You're receiving enough feedback from comments, emails, social networks, and social media news sites in order to adapt and evolve your content to better serve the audience.

2. You're growing your audience organically thanks to social media sharing by existing audience members and earned media.

3. You're gaining enough insight into what the people in your audience need to solve their problems or satisfy their desires beyond the free education you're providing.

Once you build your MVA, then you can start to diversify into other channels and test different monetization strategies. The challenge is, the MVA isn't necessarily a number, but it's helpful to set one. Michael Stelzner, founder of Social Media Examiner, waited until he built a list of 10,000 subscribers before he tried generating revenue. For Matthew Patrick with his Game Theory show, the number was 500,000 YouTube subscribers.

YOUR CORE FAN BASE

Have you ever asked colleagues about their blog, or their podcast, or the performance of their magazine? Almost invariably, the first thing out of their mouth is about size. They talk about how many subscribers they have, how much web traffic they get, or what their total deliverable audience is.

Now don't get me wrong . . . these things are very important. I love throwing out the fact to anyone who will listen that we have about 200,000 subscribers at CMI. But I have to tell myself that size is not nearly, not even close to, as important as the passion of the core fan base.

In other words, do you have fans, or do you have a list?

Soman Chainani is best known for his children's book series *The School for Good and Evil*. The first book (which shares the name of the series) has sold more than 1.5 million copies, has been translated into 25 languages, and will soon be a major motion picture.

In talking about the launch of the book, Soman says, "My biggest goal when I wrote *The School for Good and Evil*, the way to make it a success, was not to have the most readers straight off the bat, but to have the most passionate ones . . . to this day, I spend an hour a day doing fan engagement."

For Soman, those core fans became his marketing—and one million-plus books later and a movie deal, it's worked pretty well.

What if we stopped focusing on how many, and started focusing on the specific *who*?

In interviewing Arrow Electronics' Victor Gao, we found the same thing. While the large publishing companies in the electronics media space were focusing on larger and larger numbers, Arrow believed it could deliver the very best information to smaller sections and segments of that audience.

It's probably the biggest mistake Robert and I see: marketers going after more and more, instead of focusing on a very specific audience. And then impacting that audience with amazing, consistent information that turns that engagement from like to love.

BUILD THE MODEL, THEN DIVERSIFY

Once we start to build an audience of subscribers, we can begin the measurement process.

Simply put, what is the difference between subscribers that subscribe and engage in your content versus those that do not?

Do they buy? Do they buy more? Do they stay longer as customers?

What is the exact behavior change?

According to a SiriusDecisions 2015 Buyer Survey, prospects engage in 2 to 12 interactions with vendors before making a purchase, and the larger the price of the service, the more touches are needed for closing. This means that in order for customers to trust and like us more, we need more content-based subscription options.

According to Content Marketing Institute internal company data, our magic number of subscriptions is three. That means our most profitable customers, the ones that buy the most directly from us, are generally subscribed to at least three different CMI programs. Readers might subscribe first to our email newsletter after reading our blog content. Then, they may sign up for one of our webinar series. Then, they may subscribe to our magazine *Chief Content Officer*, and then, possibly, our *This Old Marketing* podcast.

According to Topo, an account-based marketing advisory firm, a personalized customer journey takes over 20 content touches between sales, marketing, and account service. This is why the Arrow Electronics model works so well. Once we've achieved a minimum viable audience on one platform, we need to develop more content platforms to create better customers. That's why companies like Copyblogger didn't stop at the blog. In Copyblogger's case, it added a podcast network and an in-person event (among other activities) as well. The same goes for Sony's Alpha Universe (targeted to photographers), which started with a simple blog and then added a training program and a podcast series.

PROGRAM LIKE TV

Marketing expert, author, and speaker Jay Baer believes the key to this type of thinking is to program like a television network. Jay teaches, especially when it comes to social media, that marketers begin to think that it's one big thing.

"It's nearly pointless to think of social media as one thing, because the audiences, use cases, technology, algorithms, optimal cadences, and other characteristics of each social platform continue to diverge," states Baer.

What this means is that after we build our minimum viable audience, we need to launch into new platforms just like a media company would—understanding the goal, the specific audience, how we are going to measure, our publishing velocity, and the series brand (see Figure 8.1).

Figure 8.1	Jay Baer contends that brands need to look at social media planning just like a television executive would.

	f	⊙	𝕏	in	⌘
Goal (1)	Desired Outcome	Desired Outcome	Desired Outcome	Desired Outcome	Desired Outcome
Objectives (2)	Measurable Actions	Measurable Actions	Measurable Actions	Measurable Actions	Measurable Actions
Audiences (1–2)	With Whom You Are Communicating	With Whom You Are Communicating	With Whom You Are Communicating	With Whom You Are Communicating	With Whom You Are Communicating
Measurement (1–3)	How You Know It's Working (or Not)	How You Know It's Working (or Not)	How You Know It's Working (or Not)	How You Know It's Working (or Not)	How You Know It's Working (or Not)
Cadence	Expected Posts per Week	Expected Posts per Week	Expected Posts per Week	Expected Posts per Week	Expected Posts per Week
Shows (2)	Your Premier, Consistent Programming	Your Premier, Consistent Programming	Your Premier, Consistent Programming	Your Premier, Consistent Programming	Your Premier, Consistent Programming

An Example of a YouTube Channel Strategy

Yeti Perfects the YouTube Channel Strategy

Yeti, the outdoor lifestyle products manufacturer (it started with ice chests), leverages content planning to perfection with its YouTube channel. Sure, Yeti uses the platform for its new product videos, but it has more importantly carved out individual channels for specific audiences, including:

- Stories celebrating fatherhood (#MyOldMan)
- Separate channels for hunters and fishermen
- A Yeti Presents series that highlights adventurers and the country

The Three-Legged Stool Strategy

When I started in publishing 20 years ago, we used an antiquated publishing strategy called the "three-legged stool." The concept was that, in order to be the industry's leading resource and content provider, we needed to be the expert provider of information online, in print, and in person—the three legs of the stool—for our target audiences.

Funny thing is, this strategy has become the core to marketing effectiveness today for media companies and product brands involved in content. In the past, some media companies started as events or as magazines and evolved into the other areas. Today the path is pretty simple—build an audience online, and then diversify into both events and print.

Why is the three-legged stool strategy so important? What we see in most enterprises is the more we can communicate with a customer in multiple channels outside of product and service communication, that audience member generally becomes a better customer in some way.

Adding Print and Events to Digital

We are in the experiences business. We create those experiences through valuable, consistent content. While most competitors are focusing on digital experiences only, savvy brands see the opportunities offline.

Now I want you to think about the greatest content marketing examples that you know about. The Red Bulls, the Legos, the Marriotts. Do you know what they all have? You guessed it . . . they have world-class print magazines and amazing event experiences.

Of course, it's not just about print and events . . . there are so many channels for us to communicate with our audiences. But what's worked for the past 20 years are offline strategies, which are the exact ones so many marketing professionals forget about.

Today, the trusted content provider will need to continue to focus on the three key legs of the stool—online, print, and in person. If you are having trouble getting the marketing strategy you need, you may actually be missing a leg to your stool.

TWO METHODS FOR BUY-IN

In Chapter 10, Robert will take a thorough dive into how someone can start moving into this model, but it's important here to talk about two things. Throughout my years in marketing, I've seen two methods work the best when it comes to getting buy-in for new content marketing projects or additional budget.

The Pilot

As most people know, before a television show is signed on by a network, a pilot is produced. A pilot is a sampling of what's to come, which gives the network executives enough consumer feedback to know whether more episodes should be produced.

As you set out to build your minimum viable audience, if you present your plan as a pilot, you'll immediately see the key decision makers let their guard down. It's not as much of a commitment as a full-blown business model change for marketing. But as you sell the pilot, be sure to include the following:

- The length of the pilot: it should be at least 12 months.

- The overall goal of the pilot, or how the business will be different after the pilot.

- Agreed-upon metrics; if you hit them, you'll be able to move forward with "more episodes." This could be an increase in leads, more subscriptions, shorter time to close business, and/or an increase in "quality" leads, to name just a few.

Fear

When all else fails, fear can work as well as or better than a rational argument. If you show how competitors are using media to their advantage *and to your disadvantage*, you certainly ought to be able to get someone's attention.

For the "fear" plan to work, you have to do some research up front on your competition. Pick the leading marketer in your field and determine:

- How many subscribers (email, Facebook, Twitter, and so on) does it have for its content versus yours?

- How does it rank in key search terms versus your rankings?

- How does it compare in terms of social sharing?

- Is the company's online reputation positive?

- What are its recruitment activities? (Is the competitor landing the best talent?)

These are just a few items. The key in this strategy is to determine what's of critical importance to the lead decision maker and then target that argument. Clearly show how the competitor is using certain content strategies that are leaving you (and your content) exposed.

BUILD OR ACQUIRE?

In 2014, I sat in a marketing meeting with one of the largest producers of consumer goods in the world. The discussion centered on building audiences through content in various markets. In some of the markets, the company already had a solid content platform built. In others, there was nothing on the horizon.

The plan being discussed was an acquisition strategy of multiple properties where the organization would approach and, if terms were worked out, buy blogging sites and media properties that already had a built-in audience and content platform.

Sometimes it makes sense to build. Sometimes it makes sense to buy.

Expediting the Process

Blogging sites and media companies have two things that we want and need.

The first is the capability to tell stories. They have the people and processes to churn out amazing content on a consistent basis.

The second, and maybe more important, is that blogs and media sites come with built-in audiences.

Although merger and acquisition strategies have been happening ever since the first media company was launched, non-media companies are starting to get into this game recently. Photography supplies store Adorama put a buying group together when *JPG* magazine was going out of business. The group got access not only to *JPG*'s platform and content, but also to *JPG*'s 300,000 subscribers (which just happen to be Adorama's prospects and customers). And as you may recall, Arrow Electronics spent millions between 2015 and 2016 to purchase 51 media properties.

The Process of Acquiring a Content Platform

CMI purchased multiple properties to add to its platform, including a West Coast conference called Intelligent Content Conference and an awards program dubbed (fittingly) the Content Marketing Awards. We made the decision that purchasing these platforms made more sense than creating them from scratch and then competing with these properties. And to top it all off, Content Marketing Institute was then sold in 2016 to the U.K. events powerhouse UBM, which decided to acquire a platform in the content marketing space instead of building one itself.

In my previous book *Content Inc.*, I detailed the steps necessary when you are looking at purchasing an outside platform. Here's a quick review:

Step 1. Determine Your Goal

Like any good business decision, start by determining the reasons it might possibly make sense to purchase an existing content platform. Your business objectives for a purchase might include:

- To cover a geographic area that your business is currently absent from with an in-person component. The ultimate goal would be to reach more customers for cross-selling, upselling, and decreasing your customer turnover rate in that region.

- To insert your brand into the conversation around a topic you are not well known for. Let's say you manufacture a certain type of steel, and you've identified some use in the oil and gas industry. It may then make sense to look at smaller oil and gas blog sites or events and immediately become a credible part of the industry lexicon.

- To accomplish subscription objectives. Most likely, the platform will come with a built-in audience for you to nurture, grow, or leverage for cross-selling.

- To purchase the content assets themselves and the associated search engine optimization and sharing benefits with the platform.

- To acquire talent. For example, CNN purchased YouTube star Casey Neistat's video app Beme in November 2016 for $25 million primarily for the talent, not the platform.

Step 2. Clearly Identify the Audience

For this to work, you need a clear understanding of the audience gap you are trying to fill. For example, CMI targets senior-level marketers at large organizations for our magazine, *Chief Content Officer*. We target marketing, PR, social media, and SEO managers and directors (the "doers") at midmarket and larger enterprises for Content Marketing World (our event).

Step 3. Make Your Short List of Platforms

After you identify your objective and your audience, start making a list of relevant platforms that will help you meet your goals. The key is to avoid setting any limitations at this point. You can list events, blog sites, media sites, association sites, and maybe even some sites directly from your influencer list.

When you are making the list, it's handy to put it all into a spreadsheet containing relevant subscriber information such as:

- Origination date

- Current number of subscribers

- Known revenue sources (list each of them)

- Ownership structure (for example, independent blogger or media company)

For a conference or trade show, here is a list of assets we look for when purchasing an event:

- Number of attendees (past two years) with percentage of growth (or loss).

- Number of exhibitors (past two years) with percentage of growth (or loss).

- Number of media partners (past two years).

- General regional location.

- Registration cost (rate card).

- Marquee value (this is a subjective rate determining the cache for the event—a five-point scale should work just fine).

- Possibility for setting up a media platform around the event (again, something on a five-point scale is sufficient). The idea here is that there may be potential to build the event into a fully functional media platform with online content, web events, and more.

Step 4. Approach the Best Opportunity

There are two approaches I recommend, and I've seen both of them work. You can reach out to your top pick and see where the conversation goes. The issue is that you are putting all your eggs in one basket. A better option may be to approach your top three picks all at once and convey your intentions (that you are interested in purchasing their website, event, etc.).

You'll likely be amazed at the reactions you receive. Some of the operators will never have imagined that they'd be approached on a purchase. Others (probably those with a media background) will already have an exact idea of their exit strategy and what they are looking for.

The key at this point is to get discussions started so you can gauge where potential interest may lie. Worst-case scenario when approaching a possible seller that isn't interested in selling is that you now have the potential to grow a relationship from this first contact. Simply put, you never know when intentions might change, and now you have an inside track if they do.

Step 5. Determine the Purchase Value

There is a standard measure to smaller web properties and events (we will get to that in a second), but this first part is critical: figure out what the owner wants. Just like you do with your influencers, it's your job to find out what the platform owner's goals and aspirations are. Maybe it's just monetary (though this is unlikely). Perhaps the owner is looking for a new opportunity, or he or she desperately wants out of the business (many blog site owners or event owners never imagine that their project might get larger than what they can manage or might grow in a different direction than what they intended).

For example, Arrow Electronics wanted the digital platforms, while UBM wanted to keep the in-person events. They subsequently worked out a deal in which Arrow acquired ownership of the platform but still had to promote UBM's in-person events. That was all it took, and the deal was done.

As I said, there is a proper valuation process for smaller web properties and events. To do this, you both need to sign a mutual nondisclosure agreement for protection—on both sides. Then you want to request the business's profit and loss statement for the previous two years, at least. You may also need to see documentation on current sponsorship agreements and other contracts the company holds to confirm that its P&L statement can be verified. (Important note: Legal specifics can vary widely, so please consult your legal representation before you approach any opportunity.)

For website purchases, some deals are done on a "per-subscriber" basis, some on a net profit basis. In one example I personally worked on, a media deal was based on paying $1 per subscriber. In another, it was five times earnings, paid out over a two-year period. Smaller conferences generally go for around five times net profit (for example, if the annual profit of the conference is $100,000, you would pay $500,000 for the property).

Let's look at a small conference example:

Attendees: 250
Exhibitors: 20
Revenue: $400,000
Expenses: $300,000
Net profit: $100,000
General value of the business: $100,000 × 5 = $500,000

There is a bit more that goes into it, but the estimated general value of this event would be around $500,000.

Step 6. Make Your Offer

Before you make a formal offer, you want to make sure that your price is in the right ballpark and that the owner agrees to the basics of your terms. If you have that agreement, you'll need the event owner to sign a formal letter of intent (LOI). The LOI basically means that both sides agree to continue the conversation and take the relationship to the next level of the process; it's the business acquisition equivalent of getting engaged—while it's not a meaningful or legally binding act in and of itself, it serves as an official statement of your intentions. (Note: Please consult legal representation on creating an LOI.)

Step 7. Enter Final Negotiations

Now, before you sign anything, consider these final questions:

- What email and print lists are available?

- What assets are available? Videos? Blog posts? SlideShares? Conducting a full audit of the company's assets might be necessary.

- What are the social channels in use?

- Who are the prime influencers in this space that we should connect with? Request contact details and areas of expertise (if needed).

- What vendors does the company work with? Which would it recommend?

- Are the content creators employees or freelancers?

Over the following 30 to 60 days, you would be working on a formal asset purchase agreement and reviewing all the documentation to make sure all facts, figures, and discussions are accurate and verifiable. From there, contracts are signed, followed by corks being popped on your celebratory bottles of champagne.

VALUATION AND BETTER USE OF CASH

Just a few months before this book was published, I had the opportunity to sit down with two marketing executives from separate

Fortune 100 companies. The conversation revolved around making the business case internally for purchasing a media company as part of their content marketing strategy.

Both of these executives were content champions in their own companies, but they were having trouble explaining why either of their companies would "ever" consider buying a media company.

The solution? Valuation and cash.

What I discovered was that both of these companies were flush with cash and were looking for new investment vehicles. I told them about the Arrow Electronics story and how the investment Arrow made in 51 media brands added to the overall valuation of Arrow, since the media properties were profitable. Even at a low valuation of five or six times earnings, investing cash into media properties would be a smart fiscal decision, without ever bringing up the "marketing" angle.

So if you are looking for alternative "buy-in" rationale for a media marketing model and the pilot program or instilling fear doesn't work, the idea of a better use of cash just might.

IF YOU MOVE FORWARD, DON'T DABBLE

One of my favorite movies of all time is *Major League*. It's the story of the woeful Cleveland Indians baseball team making it to the playoffs against all odds.

At one point in the movie, Indians manager Lou Brown says to his team, "The local press seems to think that we'd save everyone the time and trouble if we just went out and shot ourselves."

Great motivator, that Lou Brown.

Why is this relevant every time I look at the latest Content Marketing Institute/MarketingProfs benchmark study?

Specifically, the "we'd save everyone the time and trouble" line.

You see, one of the golden nuggets of the research in 2017 was our findings on content marketing commitment level. Generally speaking, when looking at enterprises from around the globe, just 20 percent of all marketers responded that they were "fully committed" to content marketing.

This is important because those 20 percent were the most strategic, most mature, and most successful with their content marketing approaches. Commitment level predicts content marketing success.

You may ask what the other 80 percent are doing when it comes to them *not* being fully committed. The data says, to put it bluntly, wasting everyone's time.

Look, either you commit to a content business model approach or you don't. If you commit to it, chances are, over time, you'll succeed. If you don't commit, you probably won't succeed. (And most of the marketers answered "partially committed" to content marketing—what the heck does that mean? You're either pregnant or you aren't, right?)

So if you're fully committed to this approach, great. Move along.

If you're not, and you are still creating all these blogs and podcasts and white papers and e-books, you'd better take a look in the mirror. Odds are there'll be a whole lot of pain down the road for you.

And to quote another one of my favorite movies, *The Shawshank Redemption*: "Get busy living, or get busy dying." Not that marketing is life or death, but you get my meaning.

With marketing, it's all or nothing. Dabbling need not apply.

WHAT'S THE WORST THAT COULD HAPPEN?

In January I led a workshop for a group of marketers at manufacturing companies. They were all creating content in some way.

Mostly blog posts and white papers. A few e-books. One was working on a video series.

None had formally developed a strategy for any of this. Each of the programs was designed to be demand-generating activities and lead to conversions of some kind . . . mostly to sales calls. It was predictable, actually. It's what we usually see.

So let's talk about risk. All these very smart people are risking so much through execution, yet they didn't do the part of the process that actually takes no risk—the plan. I see this all the time with investors and the stock market. Through a tip or by reading an article, an investor will risk the world and execute a trade without the hint of a plan.

I get it . . . plans are boring. All the fun is in execution. And yes, all the risk.

So how do we mitigate risk? With a sensible plan that includes a strong business case with achievable goals. That means starting with one audience, focusing on one content destination, and building an audience over time. That's how every successful media company and content marketing example has started.

We know this . . . yet no one does it. We look for the quick solution, and end up spending time on content that makes little to no impact on the world.

There is someone at your organization right now that is creating content without a plan. There are people all over your company creating more and more content without a real business strategy.

Let's just say, in worst-case scenario terms, that the plan you follow from this book doesn't work. The worst-case scenario will be that you will get a handle on all the content that is being created and start to create a process that puts value on content creation. That's the worst thing that could happen.

But it's also possible that you change the world. You are about to make a bet on a different course of action than almost all other organizations in the world.

Maybe it's worth the risk.

Profitable Insights

- More valuable communication experiences with customers leads to better buying behaviors. This is why smart brands offer multiple content subscription options.

- Once an audience is built on a digital platform, consider offline platforms such as events or a print magazine.

- One of the big trends we'll see in the next 5 to 10 years will be brands purchasing media companies, as well as blogger and influencer sites.

Profitable Resources

- Amanda Todorovich, interview by Clare McDermott, February 2017.

- Brian Clark, "5 Ways Minimum Viable Audience Gives You an Unfair Business Advantage," copyblogger.com, March 14, 2014, http://www.copyblogger.com/unfair -business-advantage/.

- Eric Ries, *The Lean Startup* (Crown Business, 2011).

- Michael Stelzner, interview by Clare McDermott, January 2015.

Profitable Resources *(continued)*

- Tim Ferriss, *Tools of Titans* (Houghton Mifflin Harcourt, 2016).

- Jay Baer, "Think like a Television Network to Create a Winning Social Media Strategy," convinceandconvert.com, accessed May 26, 2017, http://www.convinceandconvert .com/social-media-strategy/think-like-a-television -network-to-create-a-winning-social-media-strategy/.

- Yeti YouTube page, accessed May 26, 2017, https:// www.youtube.com/user/YetiVideos/featured.

- Steven Fehlberg, "CNN Buys Casey Neistat's Video App Beme," cnn.com, November 28, 2016, https:// www.wsj.com/articles/cnn-buys-casey-neistats-video -app-beme-1480353128.

CHAPTER 9

What Now:
Lessons Learned Along the Transformation

BY
ROBERT
ROSE

Transformation literally means going beyond your form.

—Wayne Dyer

Sometimes not having any idea where we're going works out better than we could possibly have imagined.

—Ann Patchett, *What Now?*

So. What now? You've come from Chapter 8, and you say "I'm in." But how are we really going to transform marketing?

And let's be honest; a complete transformation of the marketing department is not going to happen by simply deciding that it should. There will be many, many people to consult with, details to work out—and evolutionary processes to follow.

In many instances these days, it all starts with the "business case," or "road map." This is typically a wonderfully drafted vision statement, followed by purpose, new organizational charts, strategic initiatives, budgets, and changed priority in the work that will be done.

And to be clear—this is important. But the critical thing is that just because this work is done, it doesn't mean the result, or the implications, will be clear. The essence of any transformation is the actual work that follows. If we truly believe that this evolution may even make some sense for part of our strategy, it will affect everything we do. It will change the way we account, to the way we sell, service, and retain customers, to the way we organize our public relations, to even our product development and research and development.

As we've said frequently, and in many ways, in this book—killing the marketing we know will be different for the 150-year-old enterprise than it will be for the newly minted startup in Silicon Valley. It may not come as one swift stroke, but may be made up of multiyear projects that span regional and even global strategies.

But there is a through-line we see in companies that, even though in different parts of their journey, are succeeding in this transformation. It is that they are willing to try. They recognize that the marketing of today is not enough and that the business must fundamentally evolve if it is to thrive.

Consider these three very different examples.

ZAPPOS

As we discussed in a previous chapter, Zappos has built a complete revenue-generating marketing platform—its Zappos Insights Program. But it isn't stopping there. It is continually developing new "products" that serve the marketing function of its business. In this interview, Christa Foley from Zappos tells us some of the challenges Zappos marketers have faced.

QUESTION: How do you look to developing new, innovative customer and content initiatives?

Christa: There are two big initiatives that we're looking to move into. The first one, which I am really excited about, targets senior leaders in our customers in a few key areas, but most specifically human resources work around culture and customer service. Now, because these customers want hear from us on these topics, we're launching what we're calling our Mentor On-Demand program.

Tony [Hsieh], our CEO, will be one of the offerings as a mentor. It's an opportunity for you, the customer, to have a call, or Skype, with one of our experts for a fee. Or, it can be an ongoing program—such as five calls with Tony over the course of six months. The customer can ask any and all things of whichever mentor or mentors they've chosen to speak with.

The second initiative that we are looking to launch is actually going back to the original focus of Zappos Insights. We want to upgrade our membership program into a digital training program, with complete curriculums and added content to our membership site. We're focused on addressing people who can't physically be here, or as a way for people who do come to an event to continue to stay up on what we're doing, how we're thinking about it, and successes and failures that we've had.

QUESTION: How do you handle scaling all these programs across a company as large as Zappos?

Christa: Yes, everyone has different jobs within Zappos, for sure, and so scaling is a challenge. But we're always very service-focused, and we would love it if other organizations would view the importance of culture in the way that we do. Hollie Delaney, who heads our HR group, is excited to do this, as is Rob Siefker, the head of our customer loyalty team. And, you know, we've built an agile process that focuses on "if something doesn't cause harm, try it." So, we will launch this, and if it becomes successful and Hollie's now slapped with 20 hours a week on calls, then we can revisit it and ask, "Great, how do we scale that? What's realistic?" But these are welcome problems to solve.

QUESTION: Things move so quickly today, with new competitors as well as new modes of operating. How does Zappos keep up with the speed of today's business?

Christa: We've seen the statistics, that only 12 percent of the Fortune 500 in 1955 remain today, and Tony has always talked about our end goal of Zappos to be around in 100 years. But that may mean something different than people thinking about shoes when they think of Zappos. Maybe they think about an airline, or other product lines. Tony frequently uses the example of Virgin as an example of a company that's done a great job of diversifying their business over the years. And so the idea is that you need to have resiliency in your organization. If, tomorrow, somebody creates something other than shoes, and everyone in the world shifts to that, you're in trouble if your only solution is shoes. So, it's really less about "how" and more about "why" you're in business in the first place.

So, my advice for other organizations does revolve around that concept of "if it doesn't cause harm, then give it a try." I think this is a trap that a lot of businesses fall into no matter what organization they are in. But you don't have to have the perfect plan, or idea laid out for how this is going to work in three years' time. We just looked at what our customers were doing—and asked ourselves—is that something that we can operationalize and add more value to. Those opportunities are within your organization.

SCHNEIDER ELECTRIC

Schneider's Energy University is but one stop on a long journey of transformation for the Schneider Electric team. In a global company the size and breadth of Schneider, this process will no doubt take years. But Susan Hartman shared some similar advice to that we heard from Christa and Zappos.

QUESTION: Are you constantly changing or evolving the Energy University content brand, and how do you prioritize what to develop?

Susan: We've really looked at improving Energy University and upgrading it into today's devices. So, the biggest thing we're attempting is to figure out how we do more mobile delivery and still be able to capture the student record. We want to enable students to take courses on their phone, or their iPad—and so that means a change to the interface, but also a change to the content. We'll need snackable versions of content, especially for C-Level people because they're not always going to sit there through a 40-minute course.

One of the things that we're not doing, interestingly, is adding physical events or revenue streams to this program. We tried both of them, and made a conscious decision that neither were something we wanted to continue. When we put a price tag on the program, we watched our usage rate drop by almost half. And we decided that we'd rather remove any barrier from having the quantity of students—because that meets the overall objective (marketing) better.

QUESTION: How do you deal with scaling the Energy University across such an enormous enterprise?

Susan: One of our biggest challenges was scaling this program, and I spent the first five years of the university making the pitch about what this program was, what it could do, and how it was valuable. I did this all over the world. And, we did small investments to translate the courses to get them started, and once the countries started to see the traction, they started adding it into their budgeting cycles year over year. So, we started out with three courses in five languages. And now, we've got hundreds of courses and we're now in our fourteenth language.

Also, one of the most important things we did was to partner with the top professional organizations that are associated with our audience. So, if you're talking about engineers, or healthcare professionals, or even hospitality, all of the top organizations in the country have endorsed or accredited the program. The key with these organizations is that many of them don't have the budget or resources to develop these kinds of programs, but they are suspicious of a brand coming in with educational materials. So, we worked closely with these groups to develop the content. You have to present the case, and explain it to them. You have to open up the discussion around your course development and the background of all the instructors. But once those professional organizations bought into what we were doing, it has helped us to achieve quite a lot in terms of success.

QUESTION: How have you maintained this program for so long, with all the pressures of today's business and how fast it moves?

Susan: The key part was having executive buy-in from the very top. Our CMO saw that this was a way for us to reach a huge audience of people. Education was something very easy for us to share—and we would receive incredible amounts of goodwill from educating people, creating brand awareness and then evolving those audiences into potential leads that came in by the millions.

The biggest shift was that you do have to get your subject matter experts, the scientists in our case, because it means they have to commit quite a number of hours of their time to answering questions, helping with course development, reviewing the courses, looking at the exams and everything that goes along with the operation of an online university.

And the key was having the flexibility to try something that we didn't know would work. I think no one really understood me when I first started to pitch it, and we didn't know whether it would work or not. I remember in the first six months when we started Data Center University, we had thousands of people that suddenly found this program organically—never mind even promoting it to anyone. We were amazed. It was like, you know, "build it and they will come."

Then, when we launched Energy University, that's when things really changed dimensionally for this program. Coming forward and really scaling this was an even bigger challenge because now we had to borrow people from other departments, and create new teams to make this happen.

But it's that willingness to try that really enabled it.

LIFE TIME FITNESS

Pilar Gerasimo is the founding editor of the company's magazine *Experience Life*, and while no longer an employee of the company, she continues to consult with the magazine and write a column. She shared her advice and thoughts about her experience in growing the marketing platform for the company.

QUESTION: How did you balance the creation of *Experience Life* magazine with the needs of traditional marketing and making money doing it?

Pilar: I should start by saying that even when the magazine was being underwritten by the company, I think many could feel and see that it was worth the price. However, there is no doubt that it was a significant cost. In the beginning, it was millions of dollars a year, that was not offset—not even close—by the advertising revenue we received.

But it grew over time. And even though the CEO had faith and committed to paying for and underwriting the magazine, I wanted to move it to profitability. I knew that if we continued to be viewed as a cost center, there would be a very limited number of resources available to us to expand and innovate. I was also concerned that if people didn't have to pay for the magazine, we would have no way to control the quality of the audience. As the company opened new clubs, we would get a raft of readers, but then our printing, production and distribution costs would rise as well.

So I could see that, one, we were going to continue to cost this company more and more money over time. And, secondly, we were just going to continue printing more and more of these 70-, 80-, 90-page magazines and sending them out into the world without any sense of who was reading them and how much they value them. Were they just getting landfilled, or thrown in the recycle bin? Or, were these audiences truly valuing them. So, the idea of "can we get paid for this magazine?" started to take root. We wanted to be careful about it, because there was some concern that we'd lose so many readers that we'd lose the advertising money as well.

So, we effectively decided that we would grandfather in any existing members. New members receive a free trial of the print magazine, and then have the option to continue receiving it and pay, or to not receive it, but have access online for free.

The most interesting thing was that we actually designed a negative opt-out, which of course is very controversial in the magazine world. We believed in the way we designed it, which was intended to be incredibly clear and convenient to opt out, and reflected the nature of the contracts that we have with our members, that would be the best option for us and them. We believed that people would be more angry if they stopped receiving the magazine, rather than discovering that they were paying a dollar for it.

We received almost no negative feedback. The vast majority chose to receive the magazine and to pay for it—which completely transformed the business model of the magazine. So, ever since we introduced it, the magazine has consistently between 85 percent and 90 percent opting in to receive it.

QUESTION: How have you scaled the magazine in a way that enables it to stay a profitable part of the business?

Pilar: The way that we receive the revenue from the magazine is through an extension of their membership dues, and that helped us get paid very easily.

So, over the years, we've really scaled that part well. We added automatic payment, automatic renewals, and that has really helped us manage the usual subscription and cost of subscriber retention that is so common with other magazines.

And, once we had the paid subscribers, it was easy to make the case that this magazine had retail value. So, getting the magazine on the newsstands at Whole Foods and Barnes & Noble wasn't a difficult business case to make, and it was a big part of our success as well.

As a consumer, you're not going to pick up, and pay for, something that looks like a marketing catalog, or be willing to subscribe to it. So, our focus on quality, and then the business model of the magazine was a key component of our ability to scale the reach of it as well.

QUESTION: How have you managed to keep this program going for such a long time given the rapidly changing environment of marketing?

Pilar: In creating the business case for the magazine, one of the primary arguments that I made was that audiences had become much more sophisticated in the past 10 or 15 years than they had been previously. Some of that really had to do with the rise of the internet. There was a book that had been very popular in the late nineties, I think, called *The Cluetrain Manifesto*, that described in great detail the frustration that audiences were feeling with corporate marketers just hammering them with features and benefits and prattling on about their own wonderfulness and expecting people to just buy it. Because increasingly, people were getting online and talking to each other and kind of making fun of corporate speak and self-aggrandizement. Marketers were frequently talking down to audiences as though they were stupid.

And I think everyone recognized the truth of that, but it was not a message that had really entered Life Time Fitness up until that time. One of the values and curses I brought to the company was that I was an outsider and I often would advocate for points of view or raise points that were unfamiliar and in some cases uncomfortable to consider. But, they listened and were willing to change. And, sometimes when I would speak people would recognize the truth of them. And the argument of adding value to the consumers we were serving was very difficult to deny because we all had that experience as consumers, of going, "This just sounds so disingenuous and so inauthentic, and it sounds manipulative and silly and superficial. Talk to me like I'm a real person." Anything that wasn't a true authentic effort to address the consumer's real needs and interests and questions was going to be met with ambivalence, if not hostility and resentment. And, as a brand focused on the health of our members, we had to create a brand that was not just tolerated, but beloved.

So, the company listened, and they believed and they let us try it. And once we started producing this thing, it connected with the audience in such strong ways. We received love letters, many of which said, "thank you for being different," "thank you for addressing my real needs and issues," and "what a relief to finally find a magazine that serves my needs." And the CEO kept getting people walking up to him in clubs and telling him how much they love the magazine and why.

So I had the luck and I had the good fortune of having him get it at that level. It did not mean that both he and other executives didn't continue to challenge it. They did. Over the years, there were some very specific challenges, and pressure to bring "marketing messages" into the content. They would ask, "Will we have this event? Can you write about the event?" Or, they would suggest "We have this great person. Can you do a profile of them?" We struggled with how much to focus our success stories. For example, on members versus nonmembers, and how to handle quoting experts who lived within potentially competitive organizations versus highlighting exclusively Life Time Fitness experts.

The key in shifting the culture was simply speaking common sense, stating the obvious, which just is sometimes an unpopular thing to do, and having some data to support it about the attitudes and beliefs and values of the audience in question. And then, the third, was demonstrating it, showing precisely how important it was and the fact that they say the success of a brand is when your customers start telling you back what you had originally built into your brand blueprint.

In the end, it's really just focusing on your audience.

THE COMMITMENT TO OLD VALUES
AND NEW FLEXIBILITY

As the famous lyric from the Who's song "Won't Get Fooled Again" goes, *"Meet the new boss, same as the old boss."* Our boss has always been, and will always be, the customer. The key component that we see across all three of these examples, and so many others, is the willingness to flex and adapt to new kinds of business models. The classic "that's not the way we do business" is challenged with a new model, and new ideas are tried—not as campaigns but as investments into new ways to deliver value to customers. That's the critical component of this new media marketing model—and it's no different than the old one. As we said before when we quoted Philip Kotler: CCDVTP—Create, Communicate, and Deliver Value to a Target at a Profit.

And Pilar really summed it all up beautifully at the end of her interview with us. As she was reflecting on all that she had accomplished with this new model, she said:

> We just simply have an opportunity to do something that cannot be done by a conventional media company. And I continue to think that that's the biggest opportunity in so-called content marketing. It really is just content innovation. Do the things that the conventional media company cannot do or cannot afford to do under their current business model, and leverage the opportunity you have to build a profound relationship with your customer on the basis of meeting an unmet need and speaking a truth that otherwise can't be spoken.

In many ways, the enterprise just needs to commit to being flexible to evolve new ideas of marketing. But can we? Can we be both committed to what we are doing and flexible to turning everything upside down?

We certainly make choices against the two ends of this scale almost daily. Are you committed to that route you take to work every day, or are you going to be flexible and listen to Google Maps today when it suggests a more optimal route? What about the company you take that dreaded route to every day—are you committed to that job, or are you flexible enough to consider other opportunities that come your way? How long is your business going to stay committed to your current content strategy before flexing?

There are no right answers, and as you can read in these interviews, either extreme can work against you. At one end of the scale, where commitment calcifies into habit, you may miss out on opportunities. If Pilar hadn't pushed *herself* to evolve *Experience Life* into a paid model, she might have had permission from the company to do this marketing magazine until it died an atrophied death from cost increases.

At the other end, where flexibility devolves into vacillation, you may not get much done. It would be easy for Christa to try new things constantly and quit them because of the commitments needed by the organization. But she didn't. Her team flexes and the look at how to scale things.

At the same time, either end of the scale—commitment or flexibility—can be a virtue. Sometimes to succeed we have to stay true to a course that we've committed to, maybe even beyond sensibleness. As philosopher William James once said, "Often enough our faith beforehand in an uncertified result is the only thing that makes the result come true." On the other hand, sometimes to succeed we have to flex off course. As Salesforce.com CEO Marc Benioff has said, "You must always be able to predict what's next and then have the flexibility to evolve."

How does your company choose whether to stay the course or veer off? It takes an honest look at your strengths, talents, habits, and weaknesses. A company entrenched in commitments may need to consider flexing. A company whose flexibility diminishes productivity may need to lock in on some commitments.

This honest look is especially important for us marketing change agents. Decisions to commit or flex abound for us because we are now considering things that have never been done before. We are looking at new strategies for marketing, new ways of driving revenue, new talents we will need to hire and acquire, and even new business cultures. Insight into making these decisions may come from multiple places: data, gut instinct, a passion, a belief, a philosophy, or a what-the-f toss of the dice. It's up to us to weigh commitment against flexibility. Over and over. This is the thing that will never be replaced by artificial intelligence or automation. This is our art as business strategists.

Because the future is here.

Profitable Insights

- Killing the marketing we know will be very different for the 150-year-old enterprise than it will for the startup in Silicon Valley. The one through-line that every successful company we've seen has is the willingness to try. Every company we've seen be successful at this recognizes that the marketing of today isn't enough and that the business must fundamentally evolve if it is to thrive.

- The primary lesson that we learned from Zappos was that it wants to be a 100-year company. But in its leader's mind, that may mean something very different in 100 years than what people think of Zappos today. As Christa Foley told us, "If tomorrow, somebody creates something other than shoes, and everyone in the world shifts to that, you're in trouble if your only solution is shoes."

- The biggest lesson we learned from Schneider Electric was delivering quality, focusing on continual excellence, and resisting the urge to expand just because you can. As Susan Hartman told us, "We decided that we'd rather move any barrier from having the quantity of students—because that meets our overall objective better."

- And Pilar Gerasimo from *Experience Life* relayed a wonderful lesson in developing cash from your marketing program. If audiences truly value the communication you are having with them—then they are willing to pay money for it. As Pilar said, "We believed that people would be more angry if they stopped receiving the magazine, rather than discovering that they were paying a dollar for it." Turns out she was right.

Profitable Resources

- Christa Foley of Zappos, interview by Claire McDermott, January 2017.

- Susan Hartman of Schneider Electric, interview by Claire McDermott, January 2017.

- Pilar Gerasimo of Life Time Fitness, interview by Claire McDermott, January 2017.

CHAPTER 10

The Future of Marketing

BY
**ROBERT
ROSE**

*I've been imitated so well I've heard people copy
my mistakes.*

—Jimi Hendrix

*The only difference between a rut and a grave is
the dimensions.*

—Ellen Glasgow

D id we kill marketing? Is it dead yet?

As you have no doubt guessed by now, despite the title
of this book, Joe and I are unabashed fans of the practice of marketing. We don't presume to want to end marketing—far from it.
**We want to see marketing change, expand, and evolve into the
strategic center of tomorrow's business model.**

I have been in marketing for approaching 30 years now, and I
have spent more time reading the history books of marketing than
I care to admit. I spend summers soaking up authors like Theodore
Levitt, Peter Drucker, Philip Kotler, Michael Porter, and Clayton

Christensen. I spend weekends diving into arcane historic case studies of companies that used a publishing model to change their entire business. Look at any of the now 200 examples in Joe's and my podcast *This Old Marketing*. Much to the dismay of my wife, I'm the guy who *doesn't* fast-forward through commercials on television. If you ever open your airline magazine and there are ads torn out—I'm the guy who tore them out, because I wanted to save them as a representation of what we're doing today as marketers.

To say that I'm proud to do what I do in marketing is an understatement. I'm absolutely in love with what I do. I love the theory, the science, the art, and the craft of marketing and media. And I am ultimately confident that the future holds the potential for amazing things for our beloved practice.

But how we get there is just as important.

In Joe's introduction to this book, he said something extraordinarily important. He said:

> Traditional advertising, direct marketing, digital marketing, and even social media are all transforming. And all of them point toward a landscape where brands go directly to consumers, rather than relying on the gatekeepers of traditional media to get there. The only thing that prevented this in the past was the difficulty of getting in front of an audience.

Now, I don't think you needed the more than 50,000 words you've consumed between that quote and this chapter to convince you that marketing is changing. We all know marketing is changing. All of our marketing heroes say it when they're interviewed. You can see it in every "Future of Marketing" article that is written:

What's the future of marketing?

The short answer is five words long: "make things worth talking about." The longer answer is that the marketer now needs to be in charge of everything the company does.

—Seth Godin, author, speaker

Marketing is definitely headed for a major transformation. If you think it has changed over the past five years, you ain't seen nothin' yet.

—John Hagel, author, founder of Deloitte's
Center for the Edge Innovation

There will be a shift from talking at the world to making the world talk. People don't necessarily want to be marketed to, so brands should look to create engagement and conversations at every consumer touch point. We aim to make everything we do a catalyst for conversation.

—Chris Brandt, CMO, Taco Bell

Owning your audience. In a world filled with incredible new tools to cultivate community, customers, consumers, and fans are more accessible than ever. Look for more direct conversations.

—Linda Boff, CMO, General Electric

Creative energy will see a shift away from agencies and towards publishers and platforms. An increasing number of the brightest creative minds will abandon standalone agencies for creative divisions of media companies and tech companies.

—Spencer Baim, Chief Strategic Officer,
Vice Media

Marketing 3.0 is evolved. In the first stage, marketing was transaction oriented, focused on how to make a sale. In the second stage, marketing became relationship oriented, how to keep a consumer coming back and buying more. In the third stage, marketing has shifted to inviting consumers to participate in the company's development of products and communications.

—Philip Kotler, author, professor

So, yes—marketing is changing and will continue to change. And much of it (at least in the self-serving selected quotes above) seems to align with what we're talking about in this book. But it's the last part of Joe's statement that means the most. The access to, and relationship with, an audience is *how* the practice will be fundamentally transformed.

GETTING OUT OF OUR OWN WAY

One of the things that ties many, if not most, of the illustrious quotes above together with some of their counterparts is the relatively common sentiment that "marketing" (as a strategic practice) is strategically ascendant in most organizations. Here is where we may slightly, and humbly, disagree with many luminaries. In the hundreds of consulting engagements, client advisories, workshops, and visits with marketing teams across the world, there is a palpable frustration with where marketing operations are as both science and art within the enterprise.

There are, frequently, disconnects between practitioner teams and CMOs. There are also, occasionally, unfounded fears that marketing is becoming less strategic in the business. And there are, almost always, true frustrations that the people on the marketing team are becoming less and less efficient and are chasing their tails when it comes to solving the big problems that face the business.

In a word—today, marketing is stuck in a rut. Marketing's future may be bright—but it needs a swift kick in the behind to get it out of its doldrums.

Consider a few recent developments:

- In January 2017, Marc Pritchard, Procter & Gamble's chief brand officer, stood up at the Interactive Advertising Bureau's annual leadership meeting and said with frustration, "*The days of giving digital a pass are over. It's time to grow up. It's time for action.*" He "*vowed to no longer pay for any digital media, ad tech companies, agencies or other suppliers for services that don't comply with its new rules.*" He went on to say, "We serve ads to consumers through a non-transparent media supply chain with spotty compliance to common standards, unreliable measurement, hidden rebates and new inventions like bot and methbot fraud."

  The digital magazine *Marketing Week* called it "the biggest marketing speech for 20 years."

- In July 2012, the Fournaise Marketing Group interviewed more than 1,200 CEOs from around the world. It found that 80 percent of CEOs don't trust the work their marketing units do.

- In 2016, a study found that 89 percent of marketers believe that their digital marketing efforts are simply not working. Seventy-one percent report that their digital programs often fail to meet their expectations.

- In 2015, Google released research that says 56 percent of digital ads are never seen.

- According to a recent American Marketing Association study, marketers' confidence in 2017 is at an all-time high at 69 out of a possible 100 points. And yet there were declining areas of confidence from even one year ago in a number of categories. Namely the confidence that their marketing team:

  - Has the right capabilities to be competitive—down 6 percent

  - Is doing the right things to drive growth—down 5 percent

  - Is investing in the customers who matter—down 13 percent

  - Understands the ROI of marketing plans—down 11 percent

  And maybe most pointedly . . .

  - Has the right operating model (people, structure, processes, and tools to be competitive)—down 8 percent

    And while this isn't as depressed this year as the others—this category is also *the lowest scoring of all their confidence metrics*—with only 26 percent of those surveyed feeling confident about this.

So—you may ask—with all the decreases in confidence across these categories, where is the total increase in confidence coming from? Well, according to the study, "*Marketers increasingly expect their organizational power and influence to grow, driven largely by the possibilities presented by new digital tools.*"

Yup, we're right back to where we were at the beginning of this book. ***For many, confidence remains in the hope that future*** *technology will somehow save us from our need to fundamentally change.*

But this frustration doesn't only lie within the realm of persuasive digital marketing. As Joe and I travel the world, we see the extreme pushback on our ideas of content and media leading the way.

Based on some of the recent headlines in many trade magazines, blogs, and even a few technology publications, one would have to assume the 100-plus companies we've worked with over the last 36 months are simply tilting at windmills. Have they somehow gotten themselves caught up in a "content marketing" cult, requiring a Don Draper-esque "4 Ps" intervention to bring them back into reality?

Let's assume for a moment that these companies are mistaken, that maybe the critics are correct. Maybe we need to honestly ask ourselves if all the brands we discussed in this book—such as Red Bull, Lego, General Electric, Johnson & Johnson, Kraft, and Visa— are just special because they have inherently interesting content and, therefore, represent the tiny fraction of companies that could actually replace traditional marketing and advertising with a new "over-hyped, buzzwordy" concept like what we're discussing here.

Well, you might be surprised to hear that we think they might be right. Maybe these companies *are* special. Maybe they are different. However, it bears mentioning that many of these companies were the "special ones" back in their earliest days. The then-new forms of mass media marketing disrupted the entire practice of marketing, as you can see:

- Kraft revolutionized the idea of sponsored content when, in 1947 with its agency J. Walter Thompson, it launched *Kraft Television Theatre*, which ran in different incarnations from 1947 to 1958.

- General Electric was one of the first to launch a completely sponsored radio show, called *General Electric Theater*, which would also move to the new technology of television in 1953. It was also one of the first companies to do major sponsorships of events like a huge exhibit at the 1893 World's Fair. Additionally, GE was an innovator in doing cosponsored advertising such as working with automotive manufacturers to do advertising about why great automobile lighting was so important.

- For LEGO, the last 15 years have been nothing but a magnificent ascent into one of the world's most powerful brands. The company was on the brink of bankruptcy in 2004, but the company's pivot into digital and content and focus on new product, process, and marketing innovation has been largely cited as saving the company. As LEGO has said, "We used to be a toy manufacturer. Now we're turning more and more into a media company to tell our story about these bricks."

So, perhaps, it's not the topic that makes these companies special—it's just their willingness to change and adapt.

But there are other pushbacks that we have found are true. Are you ready for it? Anyone who says that this new marketing model:

- Is not new

- Is difficult

- Won't produce more on our existing marketing campaigns

- Is not cheaper than advertising

is correct.

What the businesses we've talked about in this book recognize (and what others are ignoring) is the tremendous opportunity for the value of marketing to exist in creating value that transcends selling more product. This new model of marketing is not just a replacement for direct marketing campaigns; it is an evolutionary component of the overarching business strategy.

In other words, these companies are not evolving content to make marketing better—they're using content to evolve their approach to marketing to make the entire business better.

So, why not change? Well, let's look at some of those challenges.

THE BUSINESS CASE FOR TRANSFORMATION

At almost every marketing conference session or workshop I see or conduct, someone from a brand comes up to the speaker and asks the same question about transformation:

"How do I convince my boss that this is worth doing?"

To be clear, the "this" in that question is really some form of what you've just read about in this book.

But if we're honest, that question isn't really the question we want answered. As marketers we are saying, "Gee, I just read this book called *Killing Marketing*, and there are all these really interesting examples of companies doing interesting and productive things with content marketing and transforming their business— how do I convince my boss that we should do that?"

But what the boss actually hears is, "*Why should we invest in content, when that's seemingly all we do.*" The "I don't get it" look on the boss's face is basically—"*We already create a huge amount of content that costs us a big amount of money—where's the return for what you're asking for?*"

In other words, marketers are asking for a new car—and the CEO is rightly saying, *"What the hell have you been doing with all the parts that we've been buying?"*

Make no bones about it—for any CMO, VP, director, or even manager who attempts to evolve a marketing operating model to this structure, this kind of pushback is going to hit every aspect of that evolution. For as many success stories as we highlighted in this book, there will be the inevitable failures as well. Someone (gleefully it seems) recently sent us an article from the *Wall Street Journal* that questioned the efficacy of an owned media strategy leading the marketing operation. It was a story about how GoPro laid off 200 people, lost its head of content, and was "getting out of the entertainment biz."

As I said in Chapter 1—every time we invent the ship, we also invent the shipwreck. But here's the thing. When we invent the shipwreck, it's because we've invented the ship.

Whether you're a small business or a Fortune 100 global conglomerate, we're all feeling our way, exploring, on a journey together. For the last few years when we got it right, we were "early adopters" and "outliers" and "case studies." When we got it wrong? Well, nobody really heard about that. But guess what? It happens to everybody.

As we enter this era of pushback, the successes will come to those who are patient. It won't be enough to get early wins. We must sustain the effort. Those who do will still be the outliers, the case studies. The difference will be the failures. You'll start to hear more and more about them.

LET ME COUNT THE WAYS

In CMI's 2017 research across more than 3,500 marketers, we looked at those that felt that their success in content was decreasing over time. The top six answers (basically everything with more than 30 percent responding) were:

- Not enough time devoted—51 percent

- Management changes, staffing issues—48 percent

- Content creation challenges—46 percent

- Lack of a strategy (or inability to adjust)—38 percent

- Content marketing not a high enough priority—35 percent

- Content marketing budget issues—31 percent

So—just to the point made above—for those marketers that are not feeling successful with content, the main reason for the frustration is that we are in a catch-22 situation. We're so focused on creating more and more content, we feel like we don't have enough time, or budget, or we lack the business priority to focus on it. So, this is where the "you-suck-at-it" pushback then comes from senior management. Why should we invest *more* in content, when we already suck at the content we're creating?

Now—no one really says this. No, we use much more "business" language for this. As I mentioned above, we get these kinds of questions:

1. There is too much media already—how will we stand out in our industry?

2. This approach to marketing will cost more than advertising.

3. We aren't a media company—we can't create great content that builds audiences.

4. We can't tie content to revenue.

So let's first again acknowledge something. Every single one of these is true. But let's get to the heart of each one.

1. There Is Too Much Media Already— How Will We Stand Out in Our Industry?

This is also known as the "content shock" argument, where we look at the noise out there and, as if it were a thunderstorm, say, "*Well, it's just too nasty to go outside.*" But here's the thing: this storm isn't going to blow over. The "storm" of content started just after Gutenberg invented the printing press, and expanded with the invention of mass media technology such as radio, television, and now the Internet.

My answer to this question is, "What's the alternative?" Do we really expect the content "storm" to subside and for it to become less noisy? Do we really believe that direct advertising, marketing, social media, or other mechanisms for conversing with our customers will become easier or less complex over time? Yes, there is too much content in our industry. That doesn't mean we shouldn't create content. It just means we must invest the time and talent to be *great* at it.

2. This Approach to Marketing Will Cost More Than Advertising

Somewhere in the collective conscious of marketing—especially digital marketing—"advertising" became the de facto standard for how much things should cost. Any new approach that comes along is put through the same filter: *Is it cheaper or more expensive than advertising?* If it's cheaper, it must be worth doing; and if it's more expensive, it's not. The troubling thing about this question is that it assumes two things. The first thing it assumes is that "advertising" and the costs associated with it is as good as it's going to get and won't degrade any further. In other words, it may actually be true that evolving marketing into this model will be more expensive than advertising today. But what if advertising completely fails one day, and we haven't invested in any alternative form of marketing? And that brings us to the second assumption about advertising: that this approach to marketing is simply a replacement for advertising. This isn't true either. As we've seen, this model of marketing can provide other lines of value—including revenue that can add value to the entire business.

3. We Aren't a Media Company—We Can't Create Great Content That Builds Audiences

If our business was hurting, and the head of product management came to the CEO and said, "We can't create great products," how might the CEO react? What if that situation were reversed? In either case, the head of product management is looking either for a job or for someone who actually can create great products. The ability to create great products and services is *core* to our business.

So, if we're treating this evolution seriously, why would we expect anything less? The reason that this assertion is true is almost certainly because we haven't tried very hard. We haven't truly invested and/or exercised the muscle of creating great content— because we are so wrapped up in creating content that describes the value of our product.

Have we trained our folks to create great content? Have we invested in talented people who know how to create great content? Whatever the reason is, this is something that is not an objection to the approach—it's an objection to our skills within the approach.

4. We Can't Tie Content Marketing to Revenue

The short answer here is—"Then don't." There are myriad other ways to associate business value. As you saw in Chapter 9, Susan Hartman of Schneider Electric decided against revenue of the marketing model because it would decrease her audience size and harm one of her other business objectives, which was to draw in more leads and opportunities. Or as you saw with Pilar Gerasimo with Life Time Fitness, she decided to decrease her audience size by "turning on" a revenue-generating faucet. This might ultimately limit her ability to reach the widest audience she can with a "branding" message. So it's a smaller marketing program—but it's one that not only pays for itself but adds to her company's bottom line. It's a smarter business decision.

As the famous dodgeball coach Patches O'Houlihan said, "If you can dodge a wrench, you can dodge a ball." If you can tie *any* of your marketing and advertising to revenue, then you can tie content to revenue. But if we dig deeper, the real assertion here is that it's "too fuzzy" to associate with a sale—and thus it's hard to draw a straight line to revenue. Now, this may be true, but that's not an argument for why we shouldn't evolve—it's simply a challenge to our ability to measure.

THE IMMOVABLE OBJECT MEETS
THE UNSTOPPABLE FORCE

In our decade of experience with brands of all sizes, there is no shortage of innovative ideas in companies. However, a huge wealth of ideas never get a chance to be expressed. Leaders in companies often talk the talk of innovation, but they rarely walk the walk.

One senior manager in one of the largest PR agencies in the world recently told us: "We often have all-hands meetings where senior management gives a very inspirational speech, about how we must be innovative and deliver new content, and strategic social media solutions to our clients. 'We're going to change—and become a media operation for our clients,' he'll say. And then, once the speech is over, we all go back to our cubes and try to get reporters on the phone to get coverage for our clients."

Companies want their marketers to be innovative—you know, as long as they can prove the return on investment that innovative thing will have on the business. And this is where the institutional momentum gets in the way. We've been doing marketing for one way for so long, it can seem simply impossible to change.

So, how do we actually start these changes? What does the future hold for us?

START A STOPPING LIST

At the end of almost every advisory session that I do—after the people in our group have spent the entire day talking about either launching a new content initiative, evolving their current marketing strategy, or mapping the creation of a centralized, strategic content function in the business—a funny thing happens.

Someone (sometimes it's me, but most of the time it's someone who has been quiet for much of the meeting) says something like this: "Um, we should probably align our expectations with reality."

The room goes quiet. Heads nod. The realization sets in: This is going to be hard. Real people are going to have to *do* all this stuff. As the heads nod, the inevitable objections arise:

- ■ "We still have to support the sales guys with the materials they need."

- ■ "We still have to publish those four customer newsletters every week."

- ■ "We still have to update the customer-resource website."

- ■ "We still have to launch that new-product website next quarter."

Having watched groups go through this arc of realization over and over, I start these sessions—even before we get to the new initiative—by asking about all the things that the members of the content team are doing. Then I ask why they do each thing, and we list all the juicy reasons. Most of them come down to some variant of "That's the way we've always done it."

At the end of the day, when the heads nod, I trot out their list and ask, "Which of these things can you stop doing?" People look at each other. Uncomfortable laughter. "None of it. Senior management will want us to keep doing it all."

The business case we have to build now isn't why we should do the new thing. It's why we should stop doing the old thing. As business professor Michael Porter famously says, "The essence of strategy is choosing what not to do." I guarantee you that if you've bought into even 20 percent of what this book is talking about, in order to evolve your marketing operation even a slight bit—the very first thing you will have to focus on is what you're going to stop doing.

How about the newsletter that goes to 20,000 customers who don't read it? How about the resource center that no one uses? How about that display advertising that isn't working any longer, and that we're paying a 30 percent premium for?

What would happen if we just stopped? Who would miss it? What would we lose?

And then—as we close this book—there is one other question we can ask that might move us to action.

WHAT IF *WE'RE* WRONG?

In the summer of last year, just as we were starting to put some form on all these thoughts and present them publicly, a CEO came up to me after a workshop and said, "I think you're wrong." He continued:

> I don't think marketing should be a profit center; I think that's a distraction. I don't believe that most companies will use content to build audiences; I think—for most—that's impossible. I believe that the world of marketing is forever changed. People are now cynical to the content they consume, that trust is gone, and that really what we're talking about here is that it's the same old marketing as it always has been—just in a different package. We are simply going to have to be more transparent, more digital, and move faster.

I said, "*You may be right, but I really hope you aren't. I'm really not sure how to go any faster than we already are.*"

Joe and I believe that most businesses may believe exactly what this gentleman said to me. And let's pretend, for a moment, that he is right, and that none of what we've talked about in this book is true. Let's pretend that:

- Joe is wrong about what he wrote in the Introduction. We can't, or shouldn't, go directly to consumers rather than relying on the gatekeepers of traditional media to get there.

- I'm wrong about what I covered in the second chapter. It actually makes little sense for marketing to focus purely on building an audience over time so that we might be squarely in the initial consideration set when those customers are looking for a solution.

- Joe is wrong in Chapter 3. The new media business model and the new marketing business model are not the same.

- In Chapter 4 Joe is overstating the revenue models from a new marketing activity.

- I've misapplied the cost-savings models that I talked about in Chapter 5.

- Chapter 7 is wrong, and there is no media model that our brand can or should deploy as a means of making content work as a business strategy.

- Or as I just covered in Chapter 9—Schneider Electric, Zappos, and Life Time Fitness are just doing interesting product or loyalty plan development, not really evolving their marketing strategy.

Let's pretend all those things are true.

What harm could possibly come from trying?

Couldn't we look to what Christa Foley from Zappos said about Zappos's model when she advised:

> "If it doesn't cause harm, or move us backward, if it's safe enough to give it a try—we should actually give it a try."

Well, maybe it would be wasted money.

In my conversation with the CEO at the workshop, I said, tell me: Are you creating more or less content this year as opposed to last? "Without question, we are creating more," he said. "Exactly," I said. As businesses, we are creating more and more and more content—whether it's advertising, collateral, social media posts, blog posts, white papers, cat videos, or interviews with our CEO on the corporate social responsibility planning.

"So," I asked him. *"Doesn't it make sense to put your arms around this media, and get a strategic handle on it—even if only to manage the costs better? Even if you never, ever build an owned media experience, doesn't it make sense to invest in a process that looks at all the content you're creating strategically so that even if you don't want to be a media company, you still act like a media company in the way you operate content?"*

"Yes," he said. "It does."

See, thinking strategically doesn't actually cost you any more money. And perhaps it gives you the opportunity to try something that might provide a new way to look at marketing.

And now that we've come to the conclusion of this book, we hope we can agree that you *do* want to get more strategic about evolving the marketing content you are creating, distributing, and utilizing for business purposes.

Now, the only thing we may disagree about is how far you want to go and how many more benefits you might achieve down this new road.

Joe and I mentioned at the beginning of this book that we hoped you would push away the biases you have and begin to look at marketing as not just driving demand. We hoped that you'd look at it like you are a foreigner looking at a new country for the first time.

As Joe said in the Introduction, *"Ultimately, you have to make the decision to kill how you market so that you can take advantage of an entirely new model."*

Look at it this way. If Joe and I are right, even in a modest way, we may be looking at the biggest opportunity to transform our marketing and business strategy in 60 years. We started this book by wondering if we were asking the right question. What if it is, indeed, now a world where media isn't advertiser-supported. What if it's a world where media is advertiser-created?

Shakespeare once said, "The fault, dear Brutus, is not in our stars, but in ourselves, that we are underlings." As marketers who love our practice, as the business strategists of tomorrow, our future lies in our own making. And as Cassius was imploring Brutus, in order to make the future, we must take steps we sometimes think we cannot, to overthrow the tyrant that we believe controls us. Marketing has changed. Past tense. When you opened this book, you already recognized that. And so the only question that remains is, what are you going to do about it?

Welcome to the future of business. What we do with it is up to us.

Profitable Insights

■ We know that markets are changing; yet we haven't really changed marketing. Many thought leaders talk about the ascendancy of marketing as a practice—yet few really talk through how it will rise. *We* believe it will be about creating access to, and relationships with, audiences.

■ We must stop holding up the current state of marketing and advertising as the standard cost that must be beaten. The evolution of the market may simply mean that the classic way of marketing is over—and that alternatives will not be more efficient, or less expensive, than the new ways.

- It may be that those companies such as Kraft, General Electric, P&G, and Lego that have led their way into the new modes of marketing are special because they have compelling stories to tell. It may also be that they have had compelling stories to tell, for as long as they have, because they have always been willing to change their model of marketing.

- If we're wrong about everything in this book, and evolving marketing into a profit center isn't actually a reality—it still makes sense to become more strategic about your owned media strategy, even if only to get your arms around the cost of doing business in today's digital world. Thinking strategically about the use of owned media doesn't cost you any more.

Profitable Resources

- "25 Predictions for What Marketing Will Look Like in 2020," *Fast Company*, March 4, 2015, https://www.fastcompany.com/3043109/sector-forecasting/25-predictions-for-what-marketing-will-look-like-in-2020.

- Jack Neff, "P&G Tells Digital to Clean Up, Lays Down New Rules for Agencies and Ad Tech to Get Paid," *Ad Age*, January 29, 2017, http://adage.com/article/media/p-g-s-pritchard-calls-digital-grow-up-new-rules/307742/.

- Alex Kantrowitz, "56% of Digital Ads Served Are Never Seen, Says Google," *Ad Age*, December 3, 2014, http://adage.com/article/digital/56-digital-ads-served-google/296062/.

Profitable Resources *(continued)*

- AMA's Marketers' Confidence Index, January 2017.

- Evan Shellshear, "From Bankruptcy to Industry Leading Success—the LEGO Story," *Innovation Management*, accessed May 1, 2017, http://www.innovationmanagement .se/2016/07/11/from-bankruptcy-to-industry-leading -success-the-lego-story/.

- Steve Safran, "GoPro Lays Off 200, Gets Out of the Entertainment Business," AdWeek Network, November 30, 2016, http://www.adweek.com/lostremote/gopro-lays -off-200-gets-out-of-the-entertainment-biz/57934.

- Christa Foley from Zappos, interview by Claire McDermott, January 2017.

Index

ABM. *See* Account-based
  marketing
Account-based marketing (ABM),
  77–79
Ad blocking technology, 32
Adobe
  CMO.com of, 127
  Photoshop, 22
  Summit, 102
Adorama, 198
Advance Publications, 111
Advertising, 10–11, 33
  with benefactor sponsorship, 89
  click fraud, 32
  by Coca-Cola, 131
  content with, 122
  cosponsored, 232
  direct revenue from, 96–99
  optimized placement of, 146
  on platforms, 6
  PPC and, 46
  in print media, 65–66, 97
  sold by Arrow Electronics,
    35–36
  tracking of, 47
Affiliate sales, 95, 109–111
All the President's Men, 79
Alpha Universe, of Sony, 109, 192
Amazon Dash Button, 50
Amazon Prime, 20
  Foodable TV and, 103
Amazon Studios, 20
American Express, 25

American Graffiti, 4
American Marketing Association,
  230
America's Test Kitchens (ATK),
  81–82, 104
Apple, 29
The Appledore Cook Book (Parloa),
  42
Apps
  with content, 57
  by Nike, 58
Armada (Cline), 67
Arrow Electronics, 34–36, 68
  acquisitions of, 198, 201
  AspenCore of, 76–77
  B2B of, 9–10
  core fans of, 191
  as media companies, 76
  media model of, 74
  microsites of, 74
  original content of, 74–75
  total addressable market (TAM)
    for, 52
  UBM and, 201
Arrow.com, 74
AspenCore, 76–77
ATK. *See* America's Test Kitchens
Atlantic, 98
  subscriptions to, 20
Audience. *See also* Return on
  audience
  acquisition of, 197–203
  for blogs, 167

Audience (*continued*)
  of CMI, 87–88
  content and, 177
  for content marketing, 6
  of *Cosmopolitan*, 63–65
  democratization of, 11
  from e-newsletter, 177
  for Life Time Fitness, 238
  loyalty of, 27, 66, 71, 82, 83,
    141
  for media companies, 22, 111,
    167
  MVA and, 189
  in one media model, 158,
    164–174
  original content and, 20
  from platform acquisition, 199
  of Red Box, 97
  savings from, 121
  for social media, 192–193
Audience (Rohrs), 177
Auto Express, 66
Awolnation, 73

B2B. *See* Business-to-business
B2C. *See* Business-to-consumer
BabyCenter.com, 9, 54–55, 127,
    148
Baer, Jay, 192–193
Baim, Spencer, 227
Ballmer, Steve, 29
Barrett, Newt, 26
The Beatles, 63
Beebe, David, 141
"Belief in the Law of Small
    Numbers" (Kahneman and
    Tversky), 1
Bell, Kathy Button, 33–34
Beme, 199
Benefactor sponsorships, 89–90
Benioff, Marc, 221
Berg Welten, 72
Big Data, 150
Blogs. *See also* Copyblogger
  acquisition of, 197
  audience for, 167
  by CMI, 171

for content, 161
content type of, 170, 171
of DPS, 165–166
of *Huffington Post*, 164
From One Engineer to
    Another, 56, 108
Pillow Talk, 145
ProBlogger and, 165
by Sony, 109
Boff, Linda, 227
Bones, 120
Borden, Neil, 44–45
Brand, Peter, 1
"Branded Content," Cannes Lion
    Awards for, 25
Brandt, Chris, 227
BrandVoice, 99
Buffett, Warren, 87
Business statement, 160–162
Business-to-business (B2B), 8
  of Arrow Electronics, 9–10
  event planning by, 143
  original content for, 25
  strategic marketing of, 29
  Terminus and, 77
Business-to-consumer (B2C), 8
  event planning by, 143
  original content for, 25
  strategic marketing of, 29
BuyaCar, 66, 141
Buyer's journey, 108
  agility for, 151
  content touches in, 192
  event marketing and, 144–146
  in one media model, 161
  silos for, 144
BuzzFeed
  Facebook and, 177
  native advertising on, 98
  one media model of, 163
  platform of, 174
  premium content on, 103
  subscriptions to, 177
  Twitter and, 177

Campaign-focused marketing,
    48–49

Cannes Lion Awards, 25
Capital One, 25
Car Buyer, 66
Cash
    for beginning of marketing
        change, 203–204
    return on audience and, 59–60
Casper, 145
CCDVTP. *See* Create,
        Communicate, and Deliver
        Value to a Target market at
        a Profit
CCO. *See* Chief Content Officer
Chainani, Soman, 190
Channels. *See* Platforms
Charity Water, 105
Charter Communications, 111
Chicken Whisperer, 101
Chief Content Officer (CCO), 92,
        192, 199
Chili Klaus, 107
Chip1Stop, 74
Christensen, Clayton, 41
Cisco Systems, 25, 28
Clark, Brian, 108, 127, 172, 174,
        189
Cleveland Clinic, 142
    beginning of marketing
        changes at, 183–188
    The Health Hub of, 103
Cline, Ernest, 63, 67
CMI. *See* Content Marketing
        Institute
CMO Spend Survey, 30
CMO.com, 127
CNN, 199
Coca-Cola, 25
    Content 2020 of, 131
Coe, David Allan, 155
"The Concept of the Marketing
        Mix" (Borden), 44–45
Condé Nast, 141
"Considered It Solved," 34
Content. *See also* Original content
    with advertising, 122
    apps with, 57
    audience and, 177

decreasing success of, 234–238
for e-newsletters, 179
funded, 103
mission statement for, 164–172
in one media model, 158–159
premium, 102–103
scaling of, 133
sponsored, 98–99
studios, 140–141
syndicated, 104
types of, 170–172
value curve, 21, 23
value in, 133
visual model for, 69–71
Content 2020, of Coca-Cola, 131
Content distribution, 19–20
    cost of, 22
Content experiences, 82, 141, 144
    marketing for, 152–153
Content Inc. (Pulizzi), 26–27, 163,
        198
Content marketing, 32
    audience for, 6
    content tilt for, 170
    custom publishing and, 57
    revenue from, 238
Content Marketing Awards, 95, 198
Content Marketing Institute
        (CMI), 70
    advisory services by, 94
    audience of, 87–88
    blogs by, 171
    Content Marketing Awards by,
        95, 198
    content tilt of, 169–170
    e-newsletters of, 90
    event marketing by, 88–89
    Insights group at, 93
    online training program by,
        93–94
    podcasts by, 90, 91, 100
    print media by, 92
    research by, 94, 100
    revenue model of, 87–95
    sponsorships of, 100
    The Story of Content and, 125
    subscriptions to, 191–192

Content Marketing Institute
(CMI) (*continued*)
on technology, 121
UBM and, 70, 198
virtual events by, 92
webinars by, 91, 100, 192
white papers by, 91
Content Marketing World, 88–89
Content tilt, 166–170
for content marketing, 170
of custom publishing, 169
Content-as-value, 6, 9–10, 11
ContentTECH, 92
Cook's Country, 104
Copyblogger, 108
loyalty to, 127
MVA at, 189
platform of, 172
podcasts by, 192
subscriptions to, 174
Core fans, 190–191
Core story, 60
Corporate Executive Board, 129
Cosmopolitan, 63–65
mission statement of, 64
Cosponsored advertising, 232
Create, Communicate, and
Deliver Value to a
Target market at a Profit
(CCDVTP), 6, 60, 220
Cross-selling, 115
with acquired platform, 198
savings from, 126–127
Custom publishing, 25
content marketing and, 57
content tilt of, 169–170
loyalty and, 57
CVS, 165
"Cyber Monday," 99

Dash Button, of Amazon, 50
Davis, Andrew, 56, 115
Delaney, Hollie, 211–212
Delivering Happiness (Hsieh), 130
Dennis Publishing, 66, 68, 141
Digital Photography School
(DPS), 103

blogs of, 165–166
content tilt of, 167
mission statement of, 165–166
Direct revenue, 59–60
from advertising, 96–99
from donations, 104–105
from event marketing, 101–106
loyalty and, 83
from micro-funding, 105
revenue model for, 96–106
from sponsorships, 99–101
from subscriptions, 105–106
Disney, Walt, 69–71
Doan, Jenny, 109
Doctors, 2
Donations, 104–105
DPS. *See* Digital Photography
School
Dreamforce, 9
Drucker, Peter, 19, 36
Dumas, John Lee, 109–110, 171
Dyer, Wayne, 209

Economist, 68
EE Times, 76
EEM, 76
Electronic Products, 76
Email list rental
at CMI, 90–91
from subscribers, 176
Emerson, 33–34
Employee magazines, 57
Energy University, of Schneider
Electric, 54, 106, 213–215
E-newsletters, 35
audience from, 178
of CMI, 90
content for, 161–162, 179
content type of, 170, 171
of Goop, 66
of Red Box, 97
value of, 178–179
Enhance video, 119–120
Entrepreneur on Fire (EOF),
109–110, 171
platform of, 172–173
EOF. See Entrepreneur on Fire

Epic Content Marketing (Pulizzi), 3–4, 56, 82, 165
ESPN
  Mike & Mike on, 100–101
  one media model by, 162–163
  PTI on, 90, 101
  subscriptions to, 174
ESPN the Magazine, 163
Estée Lauder, 29
Event marketing, 46–47
  adding of, 194–195
  by CMI, 88–89
  direct revenue from, 101–106
  orchestration of, 143, 144–146
  by Salesforce.com, 59–60
  by Terminus, 78
  in three-legged stool, 194
Experience Life, 215–219, 221, 223
Experiences: the 7th Era of Marketing (Rose and Johnson), 4, 27, 33
Exxon Mobil, 65
  mission statement of, 64

Facebook, 24, 173
  BuzzFeed and, 177
  native advertising on, 98
  subscriptions to, 177
Fast Company, 163
Ferriss, Tim, 167
Fire Protection Engineering, 97
Fishkin, Rand, 109
Fleischer, Julie, 122
Flip My Funnel, 78–79
Flynn, Errol, 119
Fold Factory, 115
Foley, Christa, 130, 210–212, 221, 222
Food and Family, 77, 97, 121–122
Foodable TV, 103
Forbes, 99
Four "C" Investment Goals of Value, 53–60
Fournaise Marketing Group, 229
Franklin, Benjamin, 119
Freda, Fabrizio, 29

From One Engineer to Another blog, 56, 108
Funded content, 103
The Furrow Magazine, 113
F&W media, 81

Gambler's fallacy, 1
Game Theory, 112, 171, 172–173, 190
Gao, Victor, 34–36, 75–76, 191
Gartner, 30
GDPR. *See* General Data Protection Regulation
GE Reports, 25
General Data Protection Regulation (GDPR), 147–148
General Electric, 25, 27, 29, 227
General Electric Theater, 232
General Motors, 28
Gerasimo, Pilar, 215–219, 220–221, 223, 238
Get Content Get Customers (Pulizzi and Barrett), 26
GIE Media, 111
"Give You Wings," of Red Bull, 73
Glasgow, Ellen, 225
Godin, Seth, 167, 227
GoFundMe, 105
Google, 24, 229
Google Ads, 123, 126
Google Trends, 170
Goop.com, 66
GoPro, 232
Gordon, Jeff, 63
Great Recession, 25
Grove, Andy, 17
Grow, Keep, and Win framework, 122
Grow revenue, 114–115
The Guardian, 66

Hagel, John, 227
Harry Potter and the Deathly Hallows (Rowling), 155
Hartman, Susan, 54, 213–215, 223, 238

HBO Now, 20
Health Hub, of The Cleveland Clinic The, 103
Hearst, 10
    United Technical Publications of, 35
Hendrix, Jimi, 225
Hitler, Adolf, 3
Hoegledt, Lasse, 126
Hoff, Christina, 55
Hoffman, Dustin, 79
House organs, 57
"How to Cook That," 97
HP, 29
H&R Block, 99, 100
Hsieh, Tony, 112, 130, 211–212
HubSpot, 170
Huffington Post, 164

IAB. *See* Internet Advertising Bureau
IBM, 25, 28
Immelt, Jeff, 29
Inbound marketing, 170
Indirect revenue, 106–107
Indium
    From One Engineer to Another blog of, 56, 108
    win revenue of, 107–108
IndustryWeek, 68
Insights group, at CMI, 93
Instagram, 173, 177
Intel, 68
Intelligent Content Conference, 89, 198
Interactive Advertising Bureau, 229
Internet Advertising Bureau (IAB), 32
iTunes, 172, 175

James, LeBron, 68
James, William, 221
Jaworski, Bernie, 30
Jobs, Steve, 63
Joel, Billy, 139
John Deere, 6
    The Furrow Magazine of, 113

Johnson, Carla, 4, 27, 33
Johnson & Johnson, 27
    BabyCenter.com of, 9, 54–55, 127, 148
Jones, David, 129
Jyske Bank, 125–126

Kafta, Franz, 139
Kahneman, Daniel, 1, 41
Keep revenue, 113–114
Kelly, Kevin, 105
Key performance indicators (KPIs), 76
Kickstarter, 105
Klacher, Conny, 52
Kotler, Philip, 5–6, 29, 61, 220, 228
KPIs. *See* Key performance indicators
Kraft Foods
    Food and Family of, 77, 97, 121–122
    loyalty to, 125
    Online Recipes of, 122
    technology and, 122
Kraft Television Theatre, 31
Kraft/Heinz, 25, 27
KraftRecipes.com, 97
Krim, Philip, 145

Lead nurturing, 47
    slowing of, 125
The Lean Startup (Ries), 189
LEGO, 9, 25, 29
    as media company, 52, 232
LEGO Club Magazine, 113–114
The LEGO Movie, 9
Lennox, 102
Lessons learned, 209–223
    commitment to old values and new flexibility, 220–222
    by Life Time Fitness, 215–219, 223
    by Schneider Electric, 213–215, 223
    by Zappos, 210–212, 222
Letter of intent (LOI), 202–203

Life Time Fitness
  audience for, 238
  lessons learned by, 215–219, 223
Limbaugh, Rush, 163
Lincoln Electric, 68
LinkedIn, 78, 173
  native advertising on, 98
  subscriptions to, 175
Live Current Media, 108
LOI. *See* Letter of intent
L'Oreal, 108
Loyalty
  to ATK, 82
  of audience, 27, 66, 71, 82, 83, 141
  to Casper, 145
  to CMI, 95
  to Coca-Cola, 131
  to Copyblogger, 127
  custom publishing and, 57
  direct revenue and, 83
  to Disney, 69
  to Goop.com, 66
  Keep revenue and, 113–114
  to Kraft, 125
  marketing for, 51
  original content and, 21–23, 82
  to Red Bull, 51–52, 72, 131–132
  return on audience and, 57–58
  savings from, 122, 128–130
  to Zappos, 130, 211
Lucas, George, 4–5

Magazines. *See* Print media
Magnum Opus Awards, 95
Major League, 204
Makeup.com, 108
Managing Content Marketing (Pulizzi and Rose), 18–19
Marketing. *See also* Content marketing; Event marketing
  agility of, 143–144, 150–152
  beginning changes to, 183–208
  for content experiences, 152–153
  core components of change in process of, 142–152
  to core fans, 190–191
  core story for, 60
  diversifying model for, 191–192
  first steps in changing, 139–154
  future of, 225–246
  for loyalty, 51
  meaning-driven, 143, 146–150
  measuring investment in, 44–46
  new mantra for, 60–61
  new problem of 2017, 46–50
  nonresponse to customer revolution by, 140–142
  one media model for, 155–181
  origination of term, 41–43
  pilots in, 195–196
  problem of, 43–44
  real-time, 31
  savings for, 125–126
  three-legged stool for, 194
  training, at P&G, 29
Marketing: A Critical Textbook, 44
Marketing funnel
  for media companies, 134
  technology at, 140
Marketing mix, 44–45, 55–56
Marketing Performance Assessment, 45
MarketingProfs, 94
Marketo, 78
Marriott, 141
McKinsey, 51, 108
Meaning-driven marketing, 143, 146–150
Media companies, 10–11
  acquisition of, 197
  of Arrow Electronics, 35–36
  Arrow Electronics as, 76
  audience for, 22, 111, 167
  content studios of, 140–141
  Dennis Publishing as, 66, 68, 141
  Lego as, 52, 232
  marketing funnel for, 134
  Marriott as, 141

Media companies (*continued*)
mission statement of, 164
original content by, 83
Red Bull Media House as, 7–8, 59, 72
Media model, 95, 122. *See also* One media model
of Arrow Electronics, 74
revenue model for, 96–97
for savings, 119–137
Medium, 173
subscriptions to, 175
Men's Fitness, 66
Mentor On-Demand, of Zappos, 211
Merchandising rights
of Disney, 69
for *Star Wars*, 5
Michelin Guide, 129
Micro-funding, 105
Microsites, of Arrow Electronics, 74
Microsoft, 29
Minecraft of, 102
Middle men, 43–44
Mike & Mike, 100–101
Mildenhall, Jonathan, 131
"Mind of the Engineer," 74
Minecon, 102
Minecraft, 102
Minimum viable audience (MVA), 189
Minimum viable marketing, 28
Minimum viable product (MVP), 189–190
Miss Parloa's New Cook Book: A Guide to Marketing and Cooking (Parloa), 42–43
Mission statements, 64
for content, 164–172
of media companies, 164
in one media model, 164–174
Missouri Star Quilt Company, 109
Mondelez, 9
Morrissey, Brian, 71
Mossberg, Walt, 146–147
Moz, 109

MVA. See Minimum viable audience
MVP. *See* Minimum viable product

Native advertising, 31, 98–99
Neistat, Casey, 199
Netflix, 20
Foodable TV and, 103
New York Times, 68, 98
content studios of, 140–141
platform of, 174
Red Bull Media House and, 59
subscriptions to, 20, 106, 174
Wirecutter of, 111
Nike, 58
99Designs.com, 22
Nussbaum, David, 79–82, 83

O'Brien, Conan, 99
Ohanian, Alexis, 11
One media model
audience in, 158, 164–174
big-picture questions for, 157
business statement for, 160–162
content in, 158–159
distribution and measurement for, 160
by ESPN, 162–163
for marketing, 155–181
mission statements in, 164–174
platforms for, 172–174
revenue of, 174–175
strategy for, 163–164
subscriptions in, 174–179
"1,000 True Fans" (Kelly), 105
The Onion, 99, 100
Online Recipes, of Kraft Foods, 122
OPEN Forum, 25
OpenText, 126
Original content, 19–20, 82–83
of Arrow Electronics, 74–75
audience and, 20
business model for, 27
business strategy for, 26–27
cost of, 21–22
loyalty and, 21–23, 82
marketing strategy for, 25–26

marketing tactic for, 23–24
by media companies, 83
of Red Bull Media House, 72
on Yahoo!, 104
Outbrain, 145

Paltrow, Gwyneth, 66
Pardon the Interruption (PTI), 90, 101
Parloa, Maria, 41–43
Patchett, Ann, 209
Patrick, Matthew, 112, 171, 173, 190
PayPal, 99
Pay-per-click (PPC), 46
Penn Stater, 104
Penton Media, 80–81
Peppers, Don, 46
Pepsi, 9
P&G. *See* Procter & Gamble
Pilgaard, Claus, 107
Pillow Talk blog, 145
Pilots, 195–196
Pinterest, 173
   subscriptions to, 175
Pitchfork, 111
Plane crashes, 17
Platforms (channels)
   acquisition of, 198–203
   advertising on, 6
   for Life Time Fitness, 215–219
   MVA and, 189
   for one media model, 172–174
Podcasts, 13, 74
   by CMI, 90, 91, 100
   content type of, 171
   by Copyblogger, 192
   by Sony, 109
Polman, Paul, 29
Power Electronics News, 76
PPC. *See* Pay-per-click
Pre-customer database, 56–57
Premium content, 102–103
Print media. *See also* specific
      publications
   adding of, 194–195
   advertising in, 65–66, 97

budget for, 93
by CMI, 92
content type of, 171
subscriptions to, 175
in three-legged stool, 194
Prism Media, 80
Pritchard, Marc, 229
Pro Publica, 104–105
ProBlogger, 165
Procter & Gamble (P&G), 25, 68, 229
   marketing training at, 29
Profitable Insights, 12, 13, 37
   on beginning of marketing
      change, 207
   on first steps to marketing
      change, 153
   on future of marketing, 244–245
   on lessons learned, 222–223
   on one media model, 180
   on revenue model, 116
   on savings, 135
Profitable Resources, 13, 14–15, 37–39
   for beginning of marketing
      change, 207–208
   on first steps to marketing
      change, 154
   for future of marketing, 245–246
   for lessons learned, 223
   for one media model, 180–181
   for revenue model, 116–118
   on savings, 136–137
Proof of life
   in data, 143
   measurement of, 148
PTI. See Pardon the Interruption

Quantcast, 55

Rainmaker, 108
Raj, Wilson, 149
Rasmussen, Bill, 162
Rasmussen, Scott, 162
R&D. *See* Research and
      development

Ready Player One (Cline), 63
Real-time marketing, 31
Reardon, Ann, 97
Red Box, 97
Red Bull, 71–73
    "Give You Wings" of, 73
    licensing by, 72–73
    loyalty to, 51–52, 131–132
    syndicated content of, 104
Red Bull Media House, 7–8, 72
    as media companies, 59
Red Bull Music Publishing, 73
Red Bull Records, 73
Red Bull TV, 73
The Red Bulletin, 7–8, 72
Reddit, 11
    Advance Publications and, 111
Redelmeier, Don, 2
Redford, Robert, 79
Research and development
    (R&D), 34, 210
    at Kraft Foods, 77
    savings from, 127–128
Return on audience
    campaign value and, 55–57
    cash and, 59–60
    competency in, 53–55
    customer value and, 57–58
    loyalty and, 57–58
Return on customer (ROC), 46
Return on investment (ROI), 6
    analytics for, 150
    at Casper, 145
    maximization of, 49–50
    as measure of success, 49
    for real-time marketing, 31
    as wrong metric, 48
Return on marketing investment
    (ROMI), 45–46
Revenue
    from content marketing, 238
    of one media model, 174–175
    savings versus, 53
Revenue model, 87–115
    of CMI, 88–95
    for direct revenue, 96–106
    for grow revenue, 114–115

    for indirect revenue, 106–107
    for Keep revenue, 113–114
    for media model, 96–97
    Schneider Electric and, 238
    for win revenue, 107–113
Richter, Andy, 99
Ries, Eric, 189
ROC. *See* Return on customer
Rogers, Martha, 46
Rohrs, Jeff, 177
ROI. *See* Return on investment
ROMI. *See* Return on marketing
    investment
Rowling, J. K., 155
Rowse, Darren, 103, 165–166, 167

SAAS. *See* Software-as-a-service
Salesforce.com, 9
    event marketing by, 59–60
    flexibility of, 221
    R&D of, 128
    Terminus and, 78
Sandler Corporation, 105
SAS, 149
Savings
    from cross-sales, 126–127
    by decreasing sales costs,
        123–132
    from loyalty, 122, 128–130
    in marketing costs, 125–126
    media model for, 119–137
    from R&D, 127–128
    revenue versus, 53
    strategic account for, 132–134
    from upselling, 126–127
    from word-of-mouth referrals
        (WOM), 128–131
Schneider, Andy, 101
Schneider Electric
    Energy University of, 54, 106,
        213–215
    lessons learned by, 213–215,
        223
    revenue model and, 238
The School for Good and Evil
    (Chainani), 190
Schultz, Don, 51

Search engine optimization
  (SEO), 31
  with acquired platform, 199
SEO. *See* Search engine
  optimization
SEOMoz, 109
SFPE. *See* Society of Fire
  Protection Engineers
Shakespeare, William, 244
Short, Rick, 108
Siefker, Rob, 211
Silos, 133–134
  for buyer's journey, 144
SiriusDecisions, 9
  2015 Buyer Survey of, 191
*The 60-Second Super Cool Fold of
  the Week*, 115
Slate, 98
Sleepsleepsleepsleep.com, 145
Smosh. com, 173
Snapchat, 173
  subscriptions to, 175
Social media, 173–174. *See also
  specific companies*
  audience for, 192–193
  MVA and, 189
Social Media Examiner, 190
Society of Fire Protection
  Engineers (SFPE), 97
Software-as-a-service (SAAS), 128,
  174
Sony, 109, 192
Southwest Airlines, 164–165
Speedweek, 73
Sperl, Robert, 7, 8, 72
Sponsored content, 98–99
Sponsorships
  benefactor, of CMI, 89–90
  of CMI, 100
  at Content Marketing World,
    88
  direct revenue from, 99–101
  for webinars, 76
Star Wars, 5
Steiger, Paul, 105
Stelzner, Michael, 190
The Story of Content, 125

Subscriptions
  with acquired platform, 199
  from audience, 124
  to CMI, 191–192
  direct revenue from, 105–106
  to e-newsletters, 161–162
  of *Game Theory*, 112
  of GIE Media, 111
  of Moz, 109
  in one media model, 174–179
Syndicated content, 104

Taboola, 145
Taco Bell, 227
Talent, 11, 19
  with acquired platform, 199
  at Arrow Electronics, 10
  at CNN, 199
  cost of acquiring, 26
TAM. *See* Total addressable market
Tasty: The Cookbook, 103
TD Ameritrade
  thinkMoney by, 58, 114
  thinkorswim.com of, 57–58
Team Coco, of O'Brien, 99
Technology
  CMI on, 121
  Kraft and, 122
  at marketing funnel, 140
  as zero-sum game, 135
TED Talks, 163
Terminus, 77–79
Terra Mater, 72
ThinkMoney, 58, 114
Thinkorswim.com, 57–58
This Old Marketing, 90, 91, 192,
  226
Thompson, J. Walter, 31
Three-legged stool, for marketing,
  194
Time Inc., 141
Todorovich, Amanda, 142, 184
Tools of Titans (Ferriss), 167
Topo, 192
Total addressable market (TAM), 52
Trading Places, 87
Tversky, Amos, 1

Twain, Mark, 1, 183
Twin Atlantic, 73
Twitter, 132, 173
    BuzzFeed and, 177
    subscriptions to, 175

UBM, 9–10, 35
    Arrow Electronics and, 201
    CMI and, 70, 198
    "Mind of the Engineer" of, 74
Unilever, 29
Unique value proposition (UVP),
    158
United Technical Publications, 35
Upselling
    with acquired platform, 198
    savings from, 126–127
UVP. *See* Unique value proposition

Vajre, Sangram, 78–79
Van Winkle, 145
The Verge, 146
Vice, 98, 174, 227
Virgin, 212
Virilio, Paul, 17
Virtual events, by CMI, 92
Visual content model, of Disney,
    69–71

Wall Street Journal, 98
    content studios of, 141
    on GoPro, 232
    one media model of, 163
    subscriptions to, 174
Wannamaker, John, 44
Washington Post, 20
Watt-Evans, Lawrence, 105
Webinars, 123
    by CMI, 91, 100, 192
    content type of, 171
    sponsorships for, 76
The Week, 66

What Now? (Patchett), 209
White papers
    by CMI, 91
    content type of, 171
Whitman, Meg, 29
The Who, 220
Win revenue, 107–113
Wirecutter, 111
Witkowski, Trish, 115
WOM. *See* Word-of-mouth referrals
"Woman Going to Take a Break
    After Filling Out Name,
    Address on Tax Forms," 99,
    100
"Won't Get Fooled Again" (The
    Who), 220
Word-of-mouth referrals (WOM),
    128–131
WordPress, 172

Yahoo!, 104
Yeti Presents, 193
YouTube
    Chili Klaus on, 107
    CNN and, 199
    Game Theory on, 112, 171,
        172–173, 190
    "How to Cook That" on, 97
    Missouri Star Quilt Company
        on, 109
    Smosh on, 173
    subscriptions to, 176
    Yeti Presents on, 193

Zappos
    Insights, 112–113, 211
    lessons learned by, 210–212,
        222
    loyalty to, 130
    Mentor On-Demand of, 211
Zenger, Todd, 69

About the Authors

Joe Pulizzi is an entrepreneur, speaker, author, and podcaster. He's the founder of multiple startups, including the Content Marketing Institute (CMI), the leading content marketing educational resource for enterprise brands, recognized as the fastest-growing business media company by *Inc.* magazine in 2014 and 2015. CMI is responsible for producing Content Marketing World, the largest content marketing event in the world (held every September in Cleveland, Ohio), as well as the leading content marketing magazine, *Chief Content Officer*. He began using the term "content marketing" back in 2001, now the fastest-growing Internet marketing industry. CMI also offers advisory services for innovative organizations such as HP, AT&T, Petco, LinkedIn, SAP, the Gates Foundation, and many others. Content Marketing Institute was sold in June 2016 to UBM, a multibillion dollar events and media company out of London.

Joe is the winner of the 2014 John Caldwell Lifetime Achievement Award from the Content Council. Joe's third book, *Epic Content Marketing*, was named one of the "Five Must-Read Business Books of the Year" by *Fortune* magazine. His fourth book, *Content Inc.*, has been a top direct marketing bestseller since September 2015. Joe has also coauthored two other books, *Get Content Get Customers* and *Managing Content Marketing*. Joe has spoken at more than 400 locations in 16 countries advancing the practice of content marketing. He's delivered keynote speeches for events and organizations including SXSW, NAMM, *Fortune* magazine's Leadership Summit, Nestle, General Motors, Oracle, DuPont, SAP, HP, and Dell.

You can hear Joe on his podcasts, *This Old Marketing* and *Content Inc*. If you ever meet him in person, he'll be wearing orange. You can find Joe on Twitter @JoePulizzi.

Robert Rose is the founder and Chief Strategy Officer of the Content Advisory—the consulting and advisory group of the Content Marketing Institute. Robert has been helping marketers tell their story more effectively through digital media for more than 20 years. Over the last 5 years, Robert has worked with more than 500 companies of all sizes, including 15 of the Fortune 100. He's provided strategic marketing advice and counsel for global brands such as Capital One, Dell, Ernst & Young, Hewlett Packard, Microsoft, the Bill & Melinda Gates Foundation, and UPS.

Robert is the author of three books. His last, *Experiences: The 7th Era of Marketing*, was called a "treatise, and a call to arms for marketers to lead business innovation in the 21st century." His first book, *Managing Content Marketing*, with Joe Pulizzi is generally considered to be the "owner's manual" of the content marketing process. Over the last five years, Robert has spoken at more than 200 locations in 15 countries around the world. He's delivered keynote addresses for organizations including the ANA (Association of National Advertisers), American Marketing Association, Content Marketing World, Deloitte, Cisco, Adobe, Microsoft, and Michigan State University.

You can hear Robert on his weekly podcast with cohost Joe Pulizzi, *This Old Marketing*. He is also an early-stage investor in and advisor to a number of technology startups, serving on the advisory boards of a number of companies, such as Akoonu, DivvyHQ, and Tint.

Robert lives and loves in Los Angeles, California, with his beautiful wife, Elizabeth, and their amazing golden doodle, Daisy.